Feeding Families Fast

Kathleen Cannata Hanna

PHOTOS
J.D. Small

GRAPHIC DESIGN
Marilyn "Sam" Nesbitt

FOOD STYLIST
Gail Main

COVER RECIPES
Chicken Pizza, page 179, ONE DISH MAIN DISH; Apple Stack, page 43, GRAB & GO

COVER MODELS
Joe Hanna, Lisa Hanna, Barb Mansfield, Brian Mansfield, Jeremy Mansfield and Rebecca Riesdorff

PUBLISHER
GOTAGO, P.O. Box 157, Okemos, Michigan 48805-0157 • Website: www.feedingfamiliesfast.com

ISBN 0-9718706-0-8

DEDICATION

To Chris...

we celebrate new life together

THE BEGINNING

This book has had a very long journey—it started in the driveway of my good friend Lauren Zaworksi's driveway. She had this great idea to write a cookbook for 'Soccer Moms' who are constantly running around taking their kids to and from practices and games and such—having very little time to provide their family with quick, healthy, nutritious meals.

I agreed to work with her on this incredible idea...and we were off.... Trying to write a book when you are actually living the life that this book is supposed to help is not an easy task. We both had children in many activities including soccer, piano, swimming, trumpet, Boy Scouts, basketball, softball, baseball, Girl Scouts, ballet, tap dance, flute and football.

Lauren and I quickly realized that 'Soccer Moms' weren't the only ones having this feeding time crunch problem. We found that it was an issue for everyone with today's busy lifestyle. Hence the title you see on this book today!

Lauren and I plugged away for a couple of years on the project, making headway between sports, activities, and academic seasons. Family and personal issues became increasingly more important than our book project over the past year. Lauren regretfully bowed out of the book project to focus all of her energies on surviving breast cancer. Lauren is the most courageous, positive, strong-willed person I know. She was determined to lick this disease—and she did. Without her initial contributions and inspiration, this book would not be in your hands.

This special dedication is to Lauren and all women who have faced breast cancer. My hope is for a cure in our lifetimes.

Sincerely and with love,

Your dear friend Kathy

WITH SPECIAL THANKS

To my husband, Chris, thank you for believing in **all** of me and my abilities. We have traveled a rough road these past few years while this book was being put together. We have gotten through it and I am looking forward to the smoother road ahead.

To my children, Joe and Lisa, you have tasted more food than you would ever have wished to taste. From now on I will try very hard **not** to say, "Ohhhh, a little of this and a little of that..." in response to your question, "Mom, what's for dinner?"

To Jane and Tim who helped me stabilize my thought processes—I will be forever indebted to you both.

To Mom and Dad Cannata, you have backed me up in so many ways. Thank you for your encouraging words and notes. All your help has given me the confidence to continue with this project. You have no idea how much it all meant to me and how much it helped—I love you. Thanks, Mom, for being such an outstanding cook and teaching me everything I ever wanted to know about cooking in the kitchen—and, yes Mom, you will come to New York City with me! *To Mom and Dad Hanna,* your patience, support, prayer and unconditional love through these past years have been more than anyone can ask for—I love you.

To my two sisters, Cindy and Gina, thank you for loving me for the way I am! To my lawyer, *Steve Lasher,* thank you for being very patient and calm through the whole process. *To Bill and Nancy,* you both are comfort to my soul. *To John Z., Lauren, Patti and Judy,* thank you for being there when I needed you most. *To Earl,* you probably didn't think I would mention you—well, your gentle nudging, genuine concern and confidence in my ideas and my abilities have helped more than you know.

To "Sam," my designer, layout person, consultant, angel, and most of all, friend. I have had so much fun talking, working and drinking cheap coffee at BK with you. Your casual and calming disposition really helped me to relax through this project. A big thank you to *Rhoda at Schulers Books,* you always had the time to help answer questions and guide me through the "book selling" process. *Gail,* your food styling is perfect and your company even better. *J.D.,* what a small world it is, and I am so glad I ran into you! *Linda and Tom, as well as Shawn and Gretchen,* my neighbors—no one in the world can ask for better neighbors than you both. Thank you for the long driveway talks and the endless hours of editing.

And to *Richard Baldwin,* you have been a wealth of knowledge, inspiration, and non-ending source of information. Without you or your class I know I would not have written this book—thank you!

v

And most of all I thank the *BIG GUY* upstairs—without His help, guidance and forever love and forgiveness I would not be here!

I have a group of *good friends, neighbors and family* who were essential to this cookbook. These people took part in testing recipes in this book; giving hints, comments, directions, corrections, options, opinions and observations. I would like to thank them all from the bottom of my heart.

The Brennan Family

The Guy Busch Family

My Mom: Kay Cannata (Abate)

Christina Catt

The Coady Gifford Family

Sally Dishaw and Family

Linda and Tom Dufelmeier

The Izzo Family

The David and Linda Flint Family

The Hanna's: Tim, Debby, Nicole, Danielle and
    Joshua

Tom and Ann Hanna

The Jankowski Family

Eddy Jones

Lloyd, Cindy, Bryan and Kathryn Kendall

The Munson Family

The Nakfoor-Savona Family

Scott, Gina, Savannah and Sparky Patterson

The Rable Family: Andy, Cindy, Zach and Hannah

The Reisdorff Family

Shirley Saur

Lyn and Paula Scrimger

The Cleveland Connection: Cindy, Peter and
    Peaches Seebauer

Lori Stockwell

The Zaworski Family

CONTENTS

INTRODUCTION

My solution to the question, "What will I be preparing for dinner after a full day of work, school and carpooling to after school activities?" is this cookbook. **GOT 2 GO: Feeding Families Fast** is intended to help you manage and organize your cooking and eating habits quickly and easily. Getting a nutritious, home-cooked snack or meal is important for everyone. Eating out is okay once in awhile or when you're in a pinch, but nutritionally speaking it's lousy, not to mention how fast it can blow the budget (and the waistline)!

I confess that I love to cook, I love to eat, and I love to be in the kitchen—anyone's kitchen! I know that is not the case for everyone, and I personally know many people who will make a point of staying away from the kitchen as long as they can! Even though I love to cook, I still have trouble finding the time to do it. I am constantly in my mini van zooming from one location to another with kids in the back seat eating some sort of food. When we all manage to eat together as a family (which we strive to do as much as possible) the meal is simple but complete. My time in the kitchen is limited, so I must be efficient but still satisfy my family's requirements for great tasting food. I find myself constantly referring to many of the recipes in this book time and time again.

In the following pages there are helpful hints and time saving suggestions. Take a minute to read them, and they will help save you precious minutes in preparing numerous meals in the future.

I know this book will help you stay on track feeding your family whether in the car, at the game, or at the table together. **GOT 2 GO: Feeding Families Fast** will provide you with minimal effort in the kitchen, better nutrition for the family and a huge selection of recipes that will satisfy everyone's taste. Enjoy!

FEEDING FAMILIES FAST FACTS

Be **PREPARED**. Read through the recipe(s) you are planning to prepare and make sure that you have the ingredients before you start anything. Doing this will avoid taking 45 minutes to fix a 15-minute meal. For example, this happens when the recipe calls for _minute_ rice and all you have is regular rice in the pantry. My recipes are easy to read and easy to follow and consist of many items that are already in your pantry or refrigerator.

Assume in this book that all the seasonings and/or spices are dried unless noted **_BOLDLY_** that you need to use fresh. I wanted to make the recipe easy and quick, but still flavorful.

Garlic is a bold spice that can be found fresh, in a jar or powdered. When I call for fresh garlic – crushed, it is fine to use the bottled. Gilroy® minced/crushed garlic works pretty well. You can find it usually in the produce section in your grocery, near the garlic and onions. Wow, what a concept!

When you see 1–2 chicken breasts, for example, it is okay to use one large or two small etc... The recipe can handle either/or. If using a thick chicken breast (over ½" thick) adjust the cooking time appropriately. Always make sure that the juices run clear when meat is pierced through the thickest part before serving.

I have tested all the recipes with 2% milk, when calling for milk, unless otherwise specified. Butter and margarine are interchangeable in most recipes unless otherwise specified.

I have used national name brands to make it easier to find at the grocery store, simplify the recipe and avoid misinterpretation.

The prep time is considered the approximate time it takes to put the dish together before its final cook/bake/grill time. Hence the cook/bake/grill time is the approximate time right before serving. I did not factor in the phone ringing, a glass of spilled milk, your child with ten neighborhood kids at your back door wanting something to drink NOW, etc...

All oven temperatures are in degrees Fahrenheit.

Cook time for microwave is based on an 800-watt microwave.

GREAT MENU IDEAS

#1
Peanut Sauce for Pasta – PASS THE PASTA
Seasoned Green Beans – THROW-INS

#2
BBQ Salmon Fillets – 15 MINUTES DISHES
Summer Chop Pasta – PASS THE PASTA

#3
Rockin' Sockin' Soccer Sauce – PASS THE PASTA
Green Salad

#4
Chicken and Pasta – PASS THE PASTA
Super Quick Seasoned Veggies – THROW-INS

#5
Field Burgers – 15 MINUTE DISHES
Fast Skillet Pasta – PASS THE PASTA
Tarragon Carrots – THROW-INS

#6
Superb Linguine – PASS THE PASTA
Green Bean Sauté – THROW-INS

#7
Sweet & Spicy Glazed Chicken – 15 MINUTE DISHES
Better Buttered Noodles – PASS THE PASTA
Green Salad

#8
Pass for Mexico Pasta – 15 MINUTE DISHES
Green Salad

#9
Fresh Flavor Turkey Burgers – 15 MINUTE DISHES
Micro Potato – THROW-INS
Steamed Broccoli

#10
Cobb Salad Pitas -15 MINUTE DISHES
Celery and Carrot Sticks

#11
Neighborhood Chicken – FAMILY MEALS
Seasoned Biscuits – THROW-INS
Greenz and Cheese – THROW-INS

#12
Sunshine Chicken Kabobs – 30 MINUTE DISHES
Quick Potato Bake – THROW-INS
Kick'in Bean Bake – THROW-INS

#13

Fast Brunch Eggs – 30 MINUTE DISHES
Red Eye Muffins – ENERGY BOOSTERS
Fresh Fruit Bowl

#14

Incredible Tomato Tart – 30 MINUTE DISHES
Green Salad
Crusty Bread

#15

Red Beans & Rice – 30 MINUTE DISHES
Fruit or Green Salad

#16

San Antonio Pork Cutlets – 30 MINUTE DISHES
Monster Potato Pancake – THROW-INS
Fruit Salad

#17

Andrea's Cinnamon Pancakes – FAMILY MEALS
Bananas & Cream – AFTER SCHOOL SNACKS
Hot Soccer Juice – ENERGY BOOSTERS
Grilled Breakfast Sausage

#18

Baked French Toast Soufflé – FAMILY MEALS
Fruit Sticks – ENERGY BOOSTERS

#19

Awesome Sandwich – FAMILY MEALS
Sliced Veggies with Ranch Dip
Chips

#20

High Protein Tomato Soup – WARM-UPS
Green Salad
Crusty Bread

#21

Neighborhood Chicken – FAMILY MEALS
Infamous Un-tossed Salad – WARM-UPS
White Rice

#22

BLT Pie – ONE DISH MAIN DISH
Tootie Fruity Fuzzy – AFTER SCHOOL SNACKS

#23

Chicken Curry Casserole – ONE DISH MAIN DISH
Great Fruit smoothie – AFTER SCHOOL SNACK

#24

Game Winning Chowder – ONE DISH MAIN DISH
Mandarin Salad – WARM-UPS

#25

Family Meeting Pot Roast – FAMILY MEALS
Green Salad
Crusty Bread

After School Snacks

When we have after school activities or a baseball game at five o'clock in the evening, my family needs a hearty snack until I serve them dinner. The recipes in this chapter will help fill the gap before dinner.

There are many choices including snacks, beverages, smoothies, dips etc.... I have used many of these recipes as appetizers for all ages as well.

Crazy Dipping Sauce

This is a creative and easy dipping sauce you can use your imagination with. I have given you some ideas below, but you can also make up your own—get crazy!

Prep time: 5 min.	Cook time: none	Quantity: 1½ cups

½ cup low sodium soy sauce

¼ cup rice wine vinegar

3 green onions, finely chopped

2 tablespoons *fresh* lemon juice

2 teaspoons sesame oil

3 large garlic cloves, crushed*

1. In a small bowl, combine all the above ingredients and let stand for at least 15 minutes before using.
2. Dip the following in this sauce or come up with your own ideas:

   Egg rolls, fried wonton, cooked rigatoni (without sauce), cooked cheese ravioli (without sauce), boiled potato cubes, celery, carrots, cucumbers, etc.

   The selections are endless.

Use chopped or minced ready-to-use garlic in the jar for convenience.

DIPPING SAUCES

These sauces are simple to whip up and are easy to have on hand.

| Prep time: 5 min. | Cook time: none | Quantity: approx. 1½ cups |

Hot Mouth Defense Dip

1 jar (10-ounce) sweet and sour sauce (La Choy® makes a good one)

2 tablespoons hot mustard

1. In a small bowl, combine above ingredients; mix well.
2. Serve or store in refrigerator up to 2 weeks.

HINT: Great for dipping cut veggies, chicken fingers, fish sticks, or cooked and chilled rigatoni.

Nutty Dip

1 cup crunchy peanut butter

5 tablespoons maple syrup

2 tablespoons soy sauce

1. In a small bowl, combine above ingredients; whisk.
2. Serve or store in refrigerator up to 2 weeks.

HINT: Excellent with celery sticks, banana slices or apple slices.

AUNT MARG'S CHEESE BALL

My very good friend's mother made this cheese ball when I was visiting years ago. I had never seen anyone make a cheese ball before, and thought they were only available in the grocery store! Once I tasted it, I was hooked and continue to use her recipe to this day. It is quite easy, can be made at least one week in advance, and is much more delicious than store bought balls. The key is getting the cream cheese to room temperature before mixing.

> Prep time: 20 min.　　Cook time: none　　Quantity: 1 large cheese ball

3 packages (8-ounce each) cream cheese, room temperature

1 jar (2-ounce) pimento, drained and chopped

2 teaspoons garlic salt

½ cup chopped walnuts

1. In mixer, beat together cream cheese, pimento and garlic salt.
2. Using waxed paper, roll cream cheese mixture into ball and chill for 15 minutes.
3. Place chopped nuts in bowl larger than cheese ball.
4. Take chilled ball and roll in nuts, pressing nuts into ball with hands.
5. Wrap tightly with plastic wrap and store in refrigerator.
6. Serve with crackers, celery and carrots.

HINT: I have modified this recipe many different ways by adding different ingredients to the basics above. Try using ½ cup shredded crabmeat, or ¼ cup finely chopped jalapeno peppers in place of the pimento, or finely grated cheddar cheese in place of the chopped nuts. You can also make three small cheese balls with this recipe and they fit perfectly in leftover small margarine tubs!

JAZZED-UP COTTAGE CHEESE

Cottage cheese has a load of calcium in it and can be used in so many ways. Here I 'jazz it up' with some other items to make it more palatable for the younger ones and older ones, too. Just try one on for size!

Prep time: 2 min.	Cook time: none	Quantity: 2 servings

1 cup cottage cheese

1 tablespoon jam (strawberry, raspberry or grape work great)

1. Mix together and eat.

OR

1 cup cottage cheese

1 green onion, finely chopped

salt and pepper to taste

1. Mix together and eat.

OR

1 cup cottage cheese

½ container yogurt with fruit on bottom

1. Mix together and eat.

NOTE: You can run with this idea and really make up some interesting combinations!

HANNA'S CAJUN TRASH

My father-in-law makes this every Christmas and New Year's Eve when everyone gets together, plays games and eats snacks for hours. A favorite for all ages.

Prep time: 5 min.   Bake time: 350°/25 min.   Quantity: makes a big bowl

½ cup margarine

1 tablespoon parsley flakes

1 teaspoon celery salt

1 teaspoon garlic powder

½ teaspoon cayenne pepper

6 drops hot pepper sauce

3 cups Corn Chex®

3 cups Rice Chex®

1 can (2.8-ounce) french-fried onions

1 can (12-ounce) mixed nuts

1½ cups pretzels

1. Preheat oven to 350 degrees.
2. Melt margarine in microwave and place in large bowl.
3. Add parsley, celery salt, garlic powder, cayenne and hot pepper sauce to margarine in large bowl; mix well.
4. Add cereal to seasoning; stir until all pieces are coated.
5. Add remaining ingredients; mix well.
6. Bake 25 minutes; stir every 8 minutes.
7. Spread on paper towels to cool.
8. Store in airtight container.

SALSA TURKEY BALLS

Make sure you use spicy salsa so the balls really get a 'kick'!

Prep time: 10 min.	Bake time: 400°/20 min.	Quantity: 24 balls

1 pound ground turkey

⅓ cup salsa, spicy

¼ cup Italian seasoned bread crumbs

¼ cup Monterey Jack cheese, grated

3-4 green onions, chopped

1-2 cloves garlic, crushed*

1. Preheat oven to 400 degrees.
2. Combine all ingredients (not including dipping sauce); mix well.
3. Make into 24 ping-pong ball size meatballs and place on cookie sheet coated with non-stick cooking spray.
4. Bake for 20-25 minutes or until golden brown.
5. Serve with Easy Dipping Sauce.

EASY DIPPING SAUCE

¼ cup salsa mixed with ¾ cup sour cream

HINT: This recipe freezes well. Just re-heat in oven before serving.

*Use chopped or minced ready to use garlic in the jar for convenience.

INFAMOUS VEGGIE GARDEN PIZZA PIE

Did you ever want to make this recipe and couldn't remember how to make it or where to find it in a recipe book? Well here is my version of it. The kids love this pizza.

Prep time: 10 min.   Bake time: 375°/15 min.   Quantity: 8-10 servings

2 containers (8-ounce each) crescent dinner rolls

1 container (8-ounce) sour cream

1 tablespoon prepared horseradish

¼ teaspoon salt

⅛ teaspoon pepper

2 cups mushrooms, chopped

1 cup tomatoes, seeded and chopped

1 cup broccoli, chopped

½ cup green pepper, chopped

¼ cup green onion, chopped

¼ cup carrot, grated

1. Preheat oven to 375 degrees.
2. Make large rectangle out of crescent rolls in 10x15x1-inch pan. Press into bottom of pan; seal all perforations with fingers.
3. Bake 15 minutes or until crust is golden brown; cool completely. (Can be made 1 day in advance; cover and store at room temperature.)
4. While crust is cooling, combine in a small bowl sour cream, horseradish, salt and pepper; mix until smooth. (Can be stored in refrigerator 1 day in advance.)
5. Spread horseradish sauce over cooled crust and top with remaining ingredients.

HINT: Once completely assembled, this keeps well in refrigerator for at least 2 days.

EASY PIZZA SQUARES

While testing a number of recipes for this book I was having a heck of a time trying to fine tune this particular one. I brought over a few samples to my neighbors and they helped me fine-tune it. When their daughter had a high school graduation open house they loved the dish so much they asked me to make a bundle of them for the party. I considered the recipe a success when over 100 pieces were devoured by the graduation crowd in a matter of minutes!

| Prep time: 10 min. | Bake time: 375°/15 min. | Quantity: 15-20 pieces |

1 container (10-ounce) refrigerated pizza crust

2 cups mozzarella cheese, grated, divided

2 large tomatoes, sliced thinly

⅓ cup Parmesan cheese, grated

1 tablespoon dried basil

⅔ cup mayonnaise

1 clove garlic, crushed*

1. Preheat oven to 375 degrees.
2. Lightly coat 10x15-inch pan with non-stick cooking spray. Press dough into pan; seal all perforations with fingers.
3. Sprinkle dough with 1 cup of mozzarella cheese. Place tomatoes in a single layer over cheese.
4. In a small bowl, combine the other 1 cup of mozzarella cheese, Parmesan cheese, basil, mayonnaise and garlic; mix well.
5. Spoon cheese mixture over tomatoes and spread with butter knife as evenly as possible.
6. Bake for 15-20 minutes or until brown and bubbly. Pizza will have a soft crust.

*Use chopped or minced ready to use garlic in the jar for convenience.

HAM CRESCENTS

I made this recipe for the fifth grade girl's soccer team. They ate them so fast I should have doubled the batch.

Prep time: 10 min.	Bake time: 375°/13 min.	Quantity: 12 snacks

1 container (8-ounce) refrigerated crescent dinner rolls

8 slices ham; sliced thinly

5 teaspoons Dijon mustard

1¼ cups cheddar cheese, grated

1. Preheat oven to 375 degrees.
2. Unroll dough onto a flat surface. Seal perforations with fingers to make 4 separate long rectangles.
3. Distribute ham evenly over the 4 rectangles of dough and spread with mustard; sprinkle with cheese.
4. Starting at short end, roll each like a jellyroll; press edges to seal.
5. Cut each roll into 3 slices and place cut side down on cookie sheet.
6. Bake for 13-15 minutes or until golden brown.
7. Remove immediately from pan and cool on rack.

HINT: The rolls can be made, sliced and frozen on a cookie sheet. When rolls are frozen solid, remove from cookie sheet and store in a freezer type zip-top storage bag. When ready to bake, place frozen rolls on baking sheet and bake (adding 5 minutes more to the bake time).

GREAT FRUIT SMOOTHIE

Incredibly refreshing on a hot day!

| Prep time: 5 min. | Cook time: none | Quantity: 2 servings |

1 container (8-ounce) yogurt, any flavor

1 cup Cool Whip® (regular or low-fat)

1 cup fruit, cut-up

1. Put all ingredients in blender and puree.
2. Pour in tall glasses and enjoy on a hot summer day.

HINT: Great combination options: strawberries and blueberry yogurt, strawberries and lemon yogurt or raspberries and vanilla yogurt.

CHOCOLATE BANANA FROSTY

A high energy and high vitamin shake that needs no ice cream. Perfect for those old bananas when you don't have the time to make the proverbial banana bread! Great for the chocolate lover in the house.

| Prep time: 5 min. | Cook time: none | Quantity: 2 servings |

3 very ripe frozen bananas, sliced*

4 tablespoons unsweetened cocoa

1 teaspoon vanilla

2 tablespoons powdered sugar

1 cup skim milk

1. Place all ingredients in the blender and blend until smooth, about 30 seconds.
2. Serve.

*HINT: When bananas are so ripe and they are about to walk off the counter, remove skins, wrap in plastic and store in freezer. They are ready to use (frozen or thawed) as directed in recipes such as banana bread, muffins, frozen drinks, milkshakes or the recipe above.

CREAMY MILK SHAKES

I wanted a milkshake that was thick, rich and creamy. This recipe is the ticket. It stays thick until you slurp the bottom of the glass!

| Prep time: 5 min. | Cook time: none | Quantity: 4 servings |

3 cups cold milk

1 package (3.9-ounce) instant pudding (any flavor)

2 cups vanilla ice cream

1. Place all ingredients in blender in order as listed above.
2. Cover and blend on high for 30 seconds.
3. Pour into tall glasses. Serve with straws and spoons.

HINT: Different flavors of ice cream can be used – plan on some unique results!

PINK LADIES

This is so much fun to serve to the girls after a super effort playing the game! It's not real sweet and has a very cherry taste.

Prep time: 5 min.   Cook time: none   Quantity: 4 servings

1 can (12-ounce) low-fat evaporated milk

1 can (14.5-ounce) unsweetened pitted tart cherries, drained *(frozen)*

2 tablespoons chocolate syrup

1½ teaspoons almond extract

⅓ cup powdered sugar

10-12 ice cubes

1. Place all ingredients in blender.
2. Blend on high for 30 seconds or until rich, frothy and creamy.
3. Pour into tall glasses and serve.

HINT: For an adult drink, add your choice of flavored liquors in place of chocolate syrup.

TOOTIE FRUITY FUZZY

A great 'light weight' refreshing drink for the summer time. Nothing can be more thirst quenching and rich in vitamins. It only takes minutes to put together. I have spent many hot summer days sitting with the kids for a few minutes on the deck sipping this refreshing beverage.

Prep time: 5 min.	Cook time: none	Quantity: 4 servings

16 ounces (2 cups) chilled 100% cranberry juice

2 whole fresh bananas, ripe, cut into slices

12 medium strawberries, stems removed, cut in half

10-12 ice cubes

1. Place all ingredients in blender.
2. Blend for approximately 30 seconds on high or until rich and frothy.
3. Pour into tall glasses and serve.

HINT: I have also used the flavored cranberry juices with great success.

BANANAS AND CREAM

This is real easy to put together. My kids make this and have a great snack with not a lot of effort and it's fresh, healthy, and quick.

| Prep time: 2 min. | Cook time: none | Quantity: approx. 4-6 servings |

1 can (12-ounce) frozen orange-pineapple juice concentrate, thawed

1 container (32-ounce) plain yogurt

Sliced fresh bananas

1. Whisk together juice and yogurt in large bowl.
2. Place in refrigerator until ready to serve over sliced bananas.

HINT: You can use canned fruit that has been drained if bananas are not available. Try pineapple, mandarin oranges or peaches.

FRUIT KABOBS

A very creative way to serve fresh fruit to your family.

Prep time: 10 min.   Cook time: none   Quantity: 20 kebobs

10 cups fresh fruit: strawberries, oranges, apples, bananas, pears, peaches, pineapple, blueberries, kiwi, mandarin oranges, grapes, etc.

Juice of 1 lemon*

20 bamboo skewers

Dip

1 container (16-ounce) frozen whipped topping, thawed

1 container (8-ounce) strawberry yogurt

1. Cut up fruit in large cubes and thread on skewers. *(Bananas, apples, peaches and pears will need to be dunked in lemon juice before skewering to keep from browning.)
2. Combine whipped topping and yogurt; use as a dip for the fruit.
3. Refrigerate fruit kabobs and dip until ready to serve.

FRUIT ROCKS

My mom made these on hot summer days when we were all bored and nothing seemed to satisfy us. It was always a treat to have a bowl of fruit rocks for a snack.

| Prep time: 5 min. | Freeze time: 30 min. | Quantity: as much as you like |

Seedless grapes with stems removed

Apple slices

Banana slices

Orange slices

Nectarine slices

Plum slices

1. Make sure fruit is very dry. Place fruit on cookie sheet covered with wax paper; freeze.
2. Remove fruit from tray and store in an airtight container in the freezer until ready to eat.
3. Eat frozen fruit immediately.
4. Very refreshing and adults like it too!

HINT: Slice fruit into ¼-inch – ½-inch thick slices. Slice oranges in half from north pole to south pole, then slice each half into ¼-inch thick slices on the latitude. (Didn't know you were going to get a geography refresher with this book, did you?!)

FAVORITE FRUIT DIP

Kids and adults love the sweetness mixed with the fruit.

| Prep time: 10 min. | Cook time: none | Quantity: approx. 2 cups |

1 package (8-ounce) cream cheese, softened

1 cup brown sugar

1 teaspoon vanilla

½ cup chopped nuts (optional)

1. In medium bowl, cream together cream cheese, brown sugar and vanilla.
2. Add chopped nuts; mix well.
3. Chill and serve with sliced apples or pears, on strawberries, bananas...even muffins.

HINT: Use non-fat cream cheese for a fat-free alternative dessert.

RAINBOW FREEZE

Perfect on a hot day.

Prep time: 2 min.   Cook time: none   Quantity: 2 glasses

4 scoops rainbow sherbet

1 medium banana, sliced

½ cup strawberries, sliced

½ cup blueberries (optional)

1 can (12-ounce) ginger ale

1. Place 2 scoops of sherbet in each glass.
2. Evenly fill each glass with bananas, strawberries and blueberries.
3. Top off each glass with ginger ale and serve.

ENERGY BOOST PARFAIT

This is a great way for kids to eat yogurt and have fun doing it.

| Prep time: 5 min. | Cook time: none | Quantity: as many as you like |

Favorite flavor of yogurt

Favorite cereal

Favorite fruit, cut up

1. In clear tall glass, layer ¼ cup yogurt, ¼ cup cereal, and ¼ cup fruit.
2. Keep layering in this order until you reach the top of the glass.
3. Serve immediately or serve frozen!

CARAMEL APPLE DIP

Rich, creamy and easy, this is a tasty snack in the fall with fresh apples!

| Prep time: 5 min. | Microwave time: 2 min. | Quantity: 2 cups |

1 package (14-ounce) caramels

1 package (8-ounce) cream cheese, softened (low-fat works well)

1. Unwrap all the caramels and place in a medium microwaveable bowl. Microwave until caramels melt, about 1-2 minutes.
2. Stir in cream cheese until smooth.
3. Delicious served warm with apple and pear slices.

HINT: Pour over French vanilla ice cream for a luscious treat!!!

FRESH FRUIT CONE

A clever way to serve the kids some fresh fruit. The fruit is full of nutrition and the cone adds a bit of sweet and makes it easy to hold.

| Prep time: 10 min. | Cook time: none | Quantity: 4 cones |

1½ cups cut up strawberries

3 cups cut up fresh fruit: bananas, apples, cherries, grapes, kiwi, peaches, nectarines, plums etc...

4 large waffle cones

Shredded coconut or chopped nuts (optional)

1. In a blender, puree the strawberries.
2. Place waffle cones in tall glass (this makes it easier to fill cones). Fill cones with cut up fruit.
3. Drizzle with pureed strawberries.
4. Sprinkle with coconut and chopped nuts.

HINT: Try mixing vanilla yogurt with the cut up fruit before filling cones.

FROZEN FLOATS

This works well when a load of kids are in the backyard in the summer playing a pick-up game and you want to serve something refreshing and fun.

Prep time: 5 min.	Freeze time: 2-3 hrs.	Quantity: approx. 8 floats

1 can (12-ounce) grape juice, frozen concentrate

Vanilla ice cream

3-ounce paper cups

Food safe Popsicle® sticks

1. Make the grape juice with only half the water called for on the can.
2. Scoop vanilla ice cream into paper cups ⅓ full. Press ice cream firmly into the bottom of the cup.
3. Insert the stick into the ice cream and slowly fill up with the grape juice.
4. Cover quickly with foil by poking end of stick through foil.
5. Freeze until firm.

HINT: Use different flavors of ice cream and juice for an exciting change.

MACHO NACHOS

The easiest way to make nachos and the kids can do this one.

| Prep time: 5 min. | Broil time: 1 min. | Quantity: 6 servings |

1 can (16-ounce) refried beans

1 can (4-ounce) green chilies, chopped and drained

2 cups cheddar cheese, grated

1 package tortilla chips (any flavor)

1. Take a large ovenproof serving platter and spread with refried beans.
2. Sprinkle beans with chilies and any other options given below; sprinkle with cheese.
3. Broil about 4-inches away from heat source for 1-2 minutes.
4. Scoop with tortilla chips.

Optional additions

Olives, green onions, chopped red or green pepper, shredded chicken or chopped jalapenos.

HINT: Sour cream and guacamole make a nice accompaniment.

CREAM CHEESE SPREAD

An incredibly tasty cheese spread for kids and teens, and you don't have to worry about what they are eating. Let them be the creators. Just whip out the spread and provide them with the 'base' and 'sprinkle' options. Some suggestions are below.

Prep time: 5 min.	Cook time: none	Quantity: optional

Spread

1 container (8-ounce) whipped cream cheese (chive/onion works well) room temperature

½ carrot, grated

¼ cup broccoli, minced

¼ cup green peppers, minced

Base options

Pita bread

Flour tortillas

Mini bagels

Corn tortillas

Sprinkle options

Chili powder

Onion powder

Dried oregano

Shredded lettuce

1. In small bowl, combine **'Spread'** ingredients; mix well.
2. Spread on **'Base'** options and sprinkle with **'Sprinkle'** options.

QUICK BEAN DIP

Great flavor!

| Prep time: 5 min. | Cook time: none | Quantity: 1¼ cups |

1 can (15.5-ounce) kidney beans, drained

1 tablespoon vinegar

1 teaspoon chili powder

⅛ teaspoon cumin

1 tablespoon onion, finely chopped

1. Place beans, vinegar, chili powder, cumin and onion in food processor.
2. Process for 30 seconds, scraping bowl every 10 seconds.
3. Serve.

HINT: Delicious with vegetables, crackers or chips.

JAZZY CHEESE DIP

I have been making this dip for ages and have never measured the ingredients. The measurements will help, but feel free to change or modify anything in this recipe—it is very forgiving. This dish has a little 'kick' to it!

| Prep time: 5 min. | Cook time: none | Quantity: approx. 12 servings |

1 cup cottage cheese, small curd

1 package (8-ounce) cream cheese, softened

1 cup sour cream

1 can (4-ounce) green chilies, chopped and drained

1 small jalapeño pepper, chopped

1 teaspoon chili powder

½ teaspoon garlic powder

2-3 green onions, chopped

1. In food processor, combine all ingredients.
2. Process for 30 seconds, scraping bowl every 10 seconds.
3. Refrigerate until ready to serve.

HINT: Serve with pretzel sticks, crackers or seasoned pita chips. Can be refrigerated up to 2 days in advance.

HUMMUS DIP

This is a quick twist on the great hummus dip. Kids love it, especially when they don't know what is in it! If your family likes more garlic flavor, swap 1-2 cloves of garlic for the garlic powder.

Prep time: 5 min.   Cook time: none   Quantity: approx. 2 cups

2 cans (15½-ounce each) garbanzo beans, drained

6 tablespoons lemon juice

2 tablespoons sesame oil

½ teaspoon garlic powder

Pinch of salt

Pita wedges

1. Put all ingredients in food processor (***not a blender***) and process until smooth. Use on/off turns for first 10 seconds.
2. Scrape sides of bowl occasionally; blend 10 more seconds.
3. Serve with pita wedges.

HINT: Can be made and refrigerated up to 2 days in advance.

GREAT GUACAMOLE

While experimenting with recipes one Sunday afternoon I made this guacamole. A friend came over to pick up her children after a play date and ended up staying for over an hour chatting with me and finishing the whole bowl of guacamole. I think that was the testament to this recipe being in this book!

Prep time: 5 min.	Cook time: none	Quantity: approx. 2½ cups

3 large avocados, ripe

1 teaspoon lemon juice

¼ teaspoon dill

½ teaspoon garlic salt

2-4 tablespoons salsa

1 cup plain yogurt

1. Peel and seed avocados, chop coarsely.
2. In a medium bowl, combine avocado and remaining ingredients; mash with a fork and mix to desired consistency.
3. Serve chilled with chips.

SAUSAGE CON QUESO DIP

I always try to keep these ingredients on hand just in case the entire team comes over unannounced—which does happen from time to time!

| Prep time: 10 min. | Cook time: 8 min. | Quantity: 4 cups |

1 pound spicy breakfast sausage

1 pound Velveeta® (processed cheese), cut into ½-inch cubes

1 medium tomato, diced

1 can (4-ounce) green chilies, chopped and drained

Tortilla chips

1. In a large skillet over medium heat, fry sausage cooking until browned; crumble. Drain on paper towels and return sausage to skillet.
2. Add Velveeta® cubes to sausage.
3. Cook over low heat until cheese melts, stirring often, about 5 minutes.
4. Stir in tomatoes and chilies.
5. Serve warm with chips.

HINT: Can be refrigerated up to 4 days in advance and reheated in microwave. You can melt the cheese in the microwave and add to the cooked sausage to speed up the process a bit!

PIZZA DIP

The ingredient list seems long but it is quite easy and delicious. Make two at a time for a large crowd. The kids just can't seem to get enough of it.

Prep time: 15 min. Bake time: 350°/15 min. Quantity: 12 servings

1 package (8-ounce) cream cheese, softened

½ cup sour cream

⅛ teaspoon garlic powder

⅛ teaspoon ground cayenne pepper

Tomato Sauce Layer**

½ cup tomato sauce

¼ teaspoon dried oregano

¼ teaspoon salt

⅛ teaspoon garlic powder

⅛ teaspoon onion powder

Garnish Layer

½ cup artichoke hearts, chopped (optional)

¼ cup green onions, sliced

¼ cup red pepper, chopped

¼ cup black olives, sliced

½ cup mozzarella cheese, grated

½ teaspoon dried Italian seasoning

1. Preheat oven to 350 degrees.
2. Coat a 9-inch pie plate with non-stick cooking spray.
3. In a small bowl, combine cream cheese, sour cream, garlic powder and cayenne pepper; mix well until smooth; spread cream cheese mixture into bottom of prepared pan.
4. For tomato sauce layer: in a small bowl, combine tomato sauce, oregano, salt, garlic powder and onion powder; mix well.
5. Pour tomato sauce over cream cheese mixture in pie plate.
6. For garnish layer: layer remaining ingredients, as listed, on top of sauce.
7. Bake for 15-20 minutes, or until cheese is browned and bubbly.

*** If in a pinch use ½ cup of canned pizza sauce in place of the tomato sauce layer.*

HINT: Serve with crackers, pita or tortilla chips.

SOCCER BUTTER

This is a great recipe for the soccer player to make with the Soccer Dad.

Prep time: 20 min.	Cook time: none	Quantity: 10 servings

½ cup peanut butter

2 tablespoons honey

2½ tablespoons nonfat dry milk

½ cup raisins

¼ cup coconut*

1. In a small bowl, blend peanut butter and honey; gradually add nonfat milk until the mixture is stiff but still easy to handle.
2. Pull the blob out of the bowl and knead in the raisins.
3. Flatten with a rolling pin ¼-inch thick. Sprinkle with coconut and roll into a 1-inch log; chill.
4. Slice into 10 servings.

HINT: Chocolate chips can be substituted for coconut for 'chocolate soccer butter'!

POWER BALLS

Very easy, very quick, very good and very nutritious!

Prep time: 5 min.	Cook time: none	Quantity: 24-30 balls

1 cup peanut butter

1 cup non-fat dry milk powder

½ cup honey

½ cup crushed cereal, any kind

1. Mix peanut butter, honey and non-fat dry milk in medium bowl until well blended.
2. Make balls the size of walnuts and roll in crushed cereal.
3. Place on cookie sheet covered with wax paper and refrigerate until ready to eat.

HINT: This recipe freezes well.

CINNAMONY STICKY BUNS

Easy, excellent and sticky like they should be!

| Prep time: 5 min. | Bake time: 350°/20 min. | Quantity: 8 servings |

½ cup butter

¾ cup brown sugar

2 teaspoons cinnamon

1 container (16-ounce) Pillsbury Grand® biscuits

1. Preheat oven to 350 degrees.
2. Melt butter in small bowl and transfer to bottom of 9-inch round baking pan.
3. In a small bowl, combine brown sugar and cinnamon; sprinkle on top of butter round pan.
4. Arrange biscuits in a single layer on top of butter and cinnamon with sides touching.
5. Bake 20 minutes or until biscuits are golden brown.
6. Remove from oven and flip over on serving platter immediately.
7. Serve hot!

GRAB AND GO

Okay, so you have five minutes to gather everything **_and_** everyone, throw it all in the van and make it to the next practice in 15 minutes...OOOPS you forgot to feed everyone!

There are so many choices in this chapter to feed your family 'on the go'. These recipes were created and tested to 'Grab & Go'. They are perfect to take in the car. Some recipes can be prepared in five minutes; others can be prepared in advance, stored in the freezer and 'Grabbed' when needed. These recipes are fun, tasty, nutritious and convenient. I hope you enjoy them as much as I do!

Helpful items to have handy when you have to 'Grab & Go':
- Aluminum foil
- Zip-top plastic bags—assortment of sizes
- Wax paper
- Plastic wrap
- Napkins, napkins and more napkins
- Re-useable ice packs
- Coolers—assortment of sizes
- Backpack containing:
    Sharpened pencils
    Pens
    Spiral notebook
    A good paperback book to read (maybe this one!)
    More napkins

Grab and Go

CHICKEN CAESAR PITAS

This recipe is easy to make and can be wrapped and carried just about anywhere!

Prep time: 5 min.   Cook time: none   Quantity: 4-6 servings

2 **cooked** boneless skinless chicken breast halves, thinly sliced

3 cups salad greens, finely chopped

¼ cup Parmesan cheese, grated

¼ cup mayonnaise

2 tablespoons Caesar salad dressing

2-3 pita breads, cut in half

1. Mix everything together except the pita.
2. Fill the pita bread halves and go.

HINT: Italian salad dressing may be used in place of the Caesar salad dressing.

STUFFED CHICKEN CRESCENTS

Great to serve at home or 'Grab & Go'!

Prep time: 10 min.　　Bake time: 350°/20 min.　　Quantity: 4 servings

Grab and Go

3 ounces cream cheese, softened

2 tablespoons margarine, melted

2 tablespoons milk

2 cups *cooked* chicken, cut into ¼-inch–½-inch cubes

¼ teaspoon salt

⅛ teaspoon pepper

1-2 green onions, chopped

1 container (8-ounce) quick crescent rolls

1. Preheat oven to 350 degrees.
2. In a medium bowl, combine cream cheese, margarine and milk; mix until smooth. Add chicken, salt, pepper and green onion; mix well.
3. Separate crescent dough into 4 rectangles; firmly press perforations to seal. Flatten dough slightly with fingers.
4. Evenly divide the chicken mixture among the 4 rectangles; mound the mixture in the center.
5. Pull the 4 corners of dough to top center of mixture, twist slightly, and seal edges.
6. Bake on a cookie sheet 20-25 minutes or until golden brown.

HINT: If you are in a hurry, you can substitute canned white meat chicken for cooked chicken.

HAM POCKETS

Wonderful for a lunchbox, snack or quick meal. Take the time to make one or two batches at once and you will be happy when it comes time to 'Grab & Go'.

Prep time: 30 min.   Bake time: 375°/15 min.   Quantity: 8 pockets

1 package (10-ounce) frozen chopped broccoli, thawed and drained

4 ounces deli ham, finely chopped

1 bunch green onions, finely chopped

⅓ cup stuffed green olives, chopped (optional)

1½ cups Swiss or cheddar cheese, grated

1½ teaspoons savory or oregano

¼ teaspoon salt

¼ teaspoon pepper

1 pound frozen bread dough, thawed

1. Preheat oven to 375 degrees.
2. In a large bowl, combine broccoli, ham, green onions, olives, cheese and spices; mix well.
3. Cut bread dough into 8 equal pieces.
4. On a lightly floured surface roll each piece of dough out to a 6-inch square. Fill each square with ⅓ cup of ham mixture. Fold one edge over filling making a rectangle and pinch tightly closed with fingers.
5. Make 2 small slits in top of pocket for steam to escape while baking. Place pockets on lightly greased cookie sheets. Bake 15-20 minutes or until golden brown.
6. Transfer to cooling rack and cool completely.

HINT: Wrap in aluminum foil and refrigerate up to 3 days or freeze up to 2 months. Re-heat frozen pockets uncovered in 350-degree oven for 10-15 minutes.

JJ'S PIZZA SNACK

Out of the oven, room temperature or cold—these rounds work great in the car!

Prep time: 8 min.	Cook time: 400°/13 min.	Quantity: 4 servings

4 whole English muffins

1 can (12-ounce) tomato sauce

½ teaspoon basil

½ teaspoon oregano

¼ teaspoon salt

Pepper to taste

1 cup mozzarella or Monterey Jack cheese, grated

24 slices pepperoni

1. Preheat oven to 400 degrees.
2. Split the muffins open and place on a cookie sheet.
3. In a small bowl, mix tomato sauce with the basil, oregano, salt and pepper; stir well.
4. Spread 1-2 tablespoons of the sauce mixture onto each muffin; cover with grated cheese.
5. Place two pieces of pepperoni on top of each muffin.
6. Bake until cheese melts, about 13-15 minutes.

HINT: To make this even easier, use a can of pizza sauce instead of tomato sauce and spices.

APPLE STACK Featured on cover

Great for the car or the lunchbox.

Prep time: 3 min.   Cook time: none   Quantity: 1 serving

1 apple, cored

3 slices cheddar cheese, ¼-inch thick

1. Slice apple horizontally into 4 equal pieces.
2. Place slices of cheese between each layer making a stack.
3. Wrap and take.

SOCCER FUEL WRAPS

Quick and easy!

Prep time: 1 min.   Cook time: none   Quantity: 1 serving

1 flour tortilla

1 stick mozzarella cheese

1 slice of your favorite deli meat

1. Place the cheese stick on the deli meat and place it on the tortilla; roll the ingredients together.
2. This can be eaten whole like a wrap or it can be cut like a jellyroll and secured with a toothpick for bite size pieces.

KID'S BURRITO

Nice and easy!

| Prep time: 5 min. | Bake time: 350°/8-10 min. | Quantity: 10 burritos |

1 can (16-ounce) refried beans

3 cups cheddar cheese, grated

1 package (10-count) flour tortillas

1. Preheat oven to 350 degrees.
2. Spread refried beans on flour tortillas; sprinkle with grated cheese and roll.
3. Place on cookie sheet with seam side down. Bake 8-10 minutes.
4. Cool slightly—Grab and........Go!

HINT: Add a little salsa to the refried beans to make them smoother. Burrito can be topped with lettuce, tomato, onion, sour cream or salsa. This makes the burrito a little harder to 'Grab & Go' in the car but makes a great snack after school at the kitchen table!

TOM'S TURKEY ROLLS

Almost everybody has done a version of this in one way or the other, but I have found that the combination of the ingredients below work perfectly together.

Prep time: 2 min.	Bake time: none	Quantity: 4 rolls

4 – 10-inch flour tortillas

¼ cup mayonnaise

2 teaspoons horseradish

12 ounces smoked turkey, thinly sliced

4 large romaine lettuce leaves, cleaned

1. Warm tortillas ever so slightly in microwave (to prevent cracking)*.
2. In small bowl, combine mayonnaise and horseradish to make sauce.
3. Spread a thin layer of sauce evenly on tortillas; then layer turkey and lettuce on top. Roll up tightly and wrap in foil or plastic wrap.
4. Serve immediately, refrigerate or pack in cooler until ready to serve.

HINT: Adding fresh tomato is a good variation. Can be eaten immediately or stored in refrigerator up to 2 days.

*Place tortillas on a plate and cover with a paper towel sprinkled with water and microwave on high for 6-10 seconds to soften.

PIZZA POCKETS

These pockets are so easy, and freeze well. Just microwave when needed, or pack the pockets warm and eat at room temperature on the road.

| Prep time: 10 min. | Bake time: 400°/15 min. | Quantity: 4 servings |

1 container (10-ounce) refrigerated pizza dough

¼ cup pizza sauce

½ pound thinly sliced luncheon meat, ham or salami

1 cup mozzarella cheese, grated

Italian seasonings

Optional fillings

Finely chopped olives

Chopped mushrooms

Finely chopped green pepper

Finely chopped onion

1. Preheat oven to 400 degrees.
2. Unroll dough and cut into 4 even pieces; place on baking sheets.
3. Spread sauce on dough to within 1-inch of edges, top with meat, cheese and any other optional filling.
4. Sprinkle with Italian seasonings, fold short side of dough over filling and seal edges by pinching dough together.
5. Bake 15-20 minutes or until golden brown.
6. Cool completely before storing in refrigerator or freezer.

PIGGY IN A BLANKET

This is an old standby from long ago. The kids enjoy making and eating them. They are easy to take with you in the car, van, truck, etc...

Prep time: 5 min.	Bake time: 375°/10-12 min.	Quantity: 48 piggies

2 containers (8-ounce each) refrigerated crescent rolls

1 package (16-ounce) cocktail frankfurters

Ketchup, mustard and barbecue sauce for dipping

1. Preheat oven to 375 degrees.
2. Unroll 1 container of crescent rolls and make 4 rectangles (pinching seam together on each triangle).
3. Press dough out with fingers to ⅛-inch thickness, keeping the rectangle shape.
4. Cut each rectangle into 6 short strips. Roll up one frankfurter on each strip and seal seam.
5. Repeat steps 2-4 with next tube of crescent rolls.
6. Place seam sides down on cookie sheet. Bake for 10-12 minutes or until golden brown.

HINT: Try placing small slices of cheese in-between frankfurter and dough for cheesy flavor. Also, try spreading barbecue sauce on the dough before wrapping frankfurters for a zippy flavor.

SOUTHWEST CHEESY BREAD

This works great as a snack, on the go or anytime.

Prep time: 5 min.   Bake time: 375°/18 min.   Quantity: 10 slices

1 container (10-ounce) refrigerated pizza dough

1 can (4-ounce) green chilies, chopped and drained

¾ cup cheddar cheese, grated

½ cup Monterey Jack cheese, grated

½ teaspoon garlic powder

1. Preheat oven to 375 degrees.
2. Unroll dough on large cookie sheet coated with non-stick cooking spray. Press dough into 10-inch square.
3. Sprinkle chilies and both cheeses over dough, leaving ½-inch edge clean.
4. Take one 10-inch side and fold over past the middle. Take the opposite 10-inch side and fold past middle to form pocket; pinch closed making a pillow.
5. Sprinkle garlic powder over top of pillow. Bake for 18-20 minutes or until golden brown.
6. Cool for about 10 minutes and serve.

HINT: This freezes well before or after baking. Increase the baking time by 5-10 minutes if frozen.

BEEF CORNER POCKETS

Fantastic flavor. Takes a bit of up-front time but well worth it.

Prep time: 30 min.	Bake time: 400°/15 min.	Quantity: approx. 30 pockets

1 package piecrust dough (use both crusts)

⅔ pound ground beef

2 tablespoons onion, finely chopped

2 tablespoons green pepper, finely chopped

1 medium tomato, seeded and finely chopped

½ teaspoon salt

¼ teaspoon pepper

1 tablespoon cornstarch

½ cup beef broth

2 tablespoons raisins, chopped

1 tablespoon slivered almonds, chopped

1. Preheat oven to 400 degrees.
2. In a medium skillet, sauté beef until brown, over medium heat, about 8 minutes; remove from heat. Drain the fat and crumble beef; return to skillet.
3. Stir in onion, green pepper, tomato, salt, pepper, cornstarch and broth; return to heat. Stir for 3-4 minutes or until mixture begins to thicken. Add raisins and almonds and remove from heat.
4. Flatten both piecrust circles slightly on floured surface and cut 3-inch circles (re-roll scraps and cut additional circles).
5. Spoon about 1 teaspoon filling evenly onto each circle (fill all circles with filling before next step).
6. Fold each circle over to form a crescent and seal with fingers. Make slit in top of crescent for steam to escape.
7. Place on ungreased cookie sheet. Bake for 15 minutes or until golden brown.
8. Serve warm.

HINT: Freezing pockets when cooled, and then re-warming in microwave makes them another great 'Grab & Go' snack!

VARIATIONS: Use taco meat or Italian seasoned ground beef or turkey.

SPARTAN ROUNDBALLERS TRAIL MIX

Great snack to have in the car when running from music lessons to play practice.

| Prep time: 2 min. | Cook time: none | Quantity: approx. 4 cups |

1 cup salted Spanish peanuts

1 cup raisins

½ cup dried coconut flakes

½ cup dried banana chips

½ cup dried pineapple

¼ cup chocolate chips

1. Combine all ingredients and store in airtight container.

RASCAL NUTS

I have eaten these since I was a kid and finally figured out how to make these rascals.

Prep time: 5 min.   Bake time: 300°/60 min.   Quantity: 1½ cups +

1 can (15-ounce) garbanzo beans

1 teaspoon garlic powder

1 teaspoon onion powder

¾ teaspoon salt

1. Preheat oven to 300 degrees.
2. Drain beans making sure there is still dampness on them; place in medium bowl.
3. In a small bowl, combine garlic powder, onion powder and salt. Sprinkle seasonings on damp beans; toss well to coat.
4. Lay beans in a ***single layer*** on lightly greased cookie sheet.
5. Bake for 60 minutes; stir every 15 minutes.
6. The beans should be brown and crispy.
7. Cool completely on cookie sheet and store in an airtight container.

QUICK CRACKERS

Keep these snacks in the house for the kid whose stomach seems to be a bottomless pit. This recipe makes it easy for the kids to make their own snacks to take to a game, practice or nibble in the car.

Prep time: 2 min.   Bake time: none   Quantity: as many as you like

Crackers: Wheat, sesame, saltines, cheddar, etc.

Cheese: Cheddar, mozzarella, Muenster, Swiss, cream cheese, etc.

Toppings: Ham, turkey, bologna, peanut butter, green olives, black olives, pineapple chunks, bananas, apples, bacon bits, tomato slices, etc.

1. Assemble the crackers, cheese, and toppings to your liking.

HINT: A lot of these items are high in calcium and protein. Use your own imagination to do the rest.

HURRICANE TWISTERS

Packed with carbohydrates and flavor!

Prep time: 8 min.	Bake time: 375°/16 min.	Quantity: 12 twisters

2 tablespoons olive oil

2 tablespoons grated Parmesan cheese

2 tablespoons poppy seeds

2 tablespoons sesame seeds

2 cloves garlic, crushed*

1 container (11-ounce) refrigerated breadstick dough

1. Preheat oven to 375 degrees.
2. Grease an 11x17-inch cookie sheet with non-stick cooking spray**.
3. In a small bowl, combine olive oil, cheese, poppy seeds, sesame seeds and garlic.
4. Separate dough into 12 breadsticks and stretch each stick to 10-inch lengths.
5. Pick up each strip individually and twist; place on cookie sheet.
6. Spread seed mixture evenly over dough (fingers work well for this part).
7. Bake 16-18 minutes or until golden.
8. Eat warm or cooled.

HINT: Keeps well in airtight container; also freezes well.

*Use chopped or minced ready to use garlic in the jar for convenience.
**Use parchment instead for easy cleanup!

SAUSAGE ROLL

Dense and filling, this snack is great to take to practice during the dinner hour.

Prep time: 10 min.   Bake time: 350°/30 min.   Quantity: approx. 10 slices

½ pound Italian sausage, hot or mild, casing removed

1¼ cup grated cheddar cheese

¼ cup finely chopped onions

2 tablespoons finely chopped green pepper

2 tablespoons finely chopped celery

1 jalapeño pepper, finely chopped (optional)

1 (16-ounce) frozen bread dough, thawed

2 tablespoons butter, melted (optional)

1. Preheat oven to 350 degrees.
2. In a medium skillet, cook sausage on medium-high until browned, about 5 minutes. Remove sausage from pan and drain on paper towels.
3. In medium bowl combine sausage, cheese, onions, green peppers, celery and jalapeño pepper.
4. Roll out dough to a 9x16-inch rectangle on counter.
5. Spread sausage mixture evenly over dough, leaving ½-inch border. Roll up starting with long side; Pinch seam closed.
6. Transfer to large baking sheet with 1-inch sides that is ***lined with parchment.***
7. Brush with butter and bake until golden brown, 30-35 minutes.
8. Cool—serve at room temperature or cold!

THE NOT SO PLAIN PEANUT BUTTER SANDWICH

A peanut butter sandwich is healthiest when paired with nutritious toppings. Have these suggested toppings in easy reach for the kids to create their own sandwich combo. An easy way to train good eating habits.

Prep time: 3 min.	Cook time: none	Quantity: as many as you like

Slices of whole wheat bread

Peanut butter, natural or regular

Assorted toppings

Raisins

Fruit spread

Wheat germ

Shredded carrots

Dried fruit

Sunflower seeds

Coconut

Granola

Banana slices

Apple slices

Goldfish® snacks

Pretzel sticks

ENERGY BOOSTERS

This chapter is loaded with energy boosting recipes for your athlete: seasoned popcorn recipes, snack mixes, muffins and fresh fruit recipe ideas. Feeding the entire team between tournaments is a cinch when choosing a recipe out of this chapter.

Enjoy having fun with the selections in this chapter—my kids have found that they can assist or even make some of these recipes themselves—which is always helpful to me!

SEASONED PITA CHIPS

There are tons of recipes for these chips. I think this is the easiest, quickest and tastiest of all.

Prep time: 10 min.   Bake time: 350°/10 min.   Quantity: 40 chips

1 package pitas, split open

Soft spread margarine

Garlic salt

Dried parsley

1. Preheat oven to 350 degrees.
2. Spread each pita with a light layer of margarine and cut in quarters; place on cookie sheet.
3. Sprinkle with garlic salt and dried parsley.
4. Bake for 10-12 minutes until browned, watching carefully so that they don't burn.
5. Cool completely and store in airtight container up to 3 days.

HINT: This is a great snack for kids when combined with a healthy dip.

SOUP CRACKER SNACK

Quick to make, perfect to take in the car for a snack and easy to vacuum up the crumbs.

Prep time: 5 min.	Bake time: 250°/15-20 min.	Quantity: 3-4 cups

1 package (1-ounce) ranch dip mix (dry mix)

¾ cup vegetable oil

1 teaspoon dill weed

¼ teaspoon lemon pepper

¼ teaspoon garlic powder

1 package (12-ounce) oyster crackers

1. Preheat oven to 250 degrees.
2. In a large bowl, whisk dip mix and oil together; add dill, lemon pepper and garlic powder.
3. Add crackers to oil mixture; coat well.
4. Pour crackers into large baking pan and bake for 15-20 minutes; stir twice during baking.
5. Remove from oven and cool.
6. Store in airtight container or zip-top plastic bag for up to 3 weeks.

GREAT GRANOLA BAR CRUMBLE

I know you can buy granola bars and granola cereal in the grocery store, but nothing beats this recipe for the true nutty granola taste. The bars are very tender so they can be eaten as a bar or crumbled in yogurt or on top of ice cream or cereal. The crumble ideas are endless.

> Prep time: 20 min.   Bake time: 350°/20 min.   Quantity: approx. 5-6 cups

3½ cups quick oats

1 cup raisins (optional)

½ cup walnuts, chopped

⅔ cup margarine, melted

¼ cup brown sugar

¼ cup honey

1 large egg, beaten slightly

1 teaspoon vanilla

½ teaspoon salt

1. Preheat oven to 350 degrees.
2. Spread oats in 9x13-inch baking pan. Bake for 15 minutes; cool.
3. In a large bowl, combine oats, raisins and walnuts.
4. In another large bowl, combine margarine, brown sugar, honey, egg, vanilla and salt; mix well.
5. Sprinkle oat mixture over top of sugar/honey mixture; mix well.
6. Coat same 9x13-inch pan with non-stick cooking spray and press the oat mixture into pan.
7. Bake for 20 minutes.
8. Remove from oven. Slice when cooled completely.
9. Store in airtight container.

NOTE: Bars are tender and crumbly—serve on top of ice cream, yogurt, as a cereal or just as a messy but delicious bar!

Energy Boosters

CHILI POPPERS

Slightly spicy and tasty!

| Prep time: 3 min. | Cook time: 1 min. | Quantity: a bowl of popcorn |

¼ cup corn oil

1½ tablespoons chili powder

½ teaspoon salt

Pinch of sugar

1 package (3.5-ounce) microwave popcorn, popped

1. In a small microwaveable bowl, combine corn oil, chili powder, salt and sugar.
2. Microwave for 30 seconds.
3. Drizzle as evenly as you can over hot microwave popcorn; toss immediately until well combined.

HINT: Sprinkle with more chili powder and salt if you really feel like getting crazy! If you want a milder flavor, use two packages of popcorn.

POWER PACKED POPCORN

This makes a large bowl! The whole family will enjoy this while watching a movie on family night.

| Prep time: 5 min. | Bake time: 300°/15 min. | Quantity: 12 cups |

1 package (3.5-ounce) microwave popcorn, popped

2 cups unsweetened dry cereal (Cheerios® or Chex® work well)

1 cup croutons (seasoned if preferred)

1 cup pretzel sticks

½ cup dry roasted peanuts

2 tablespoons butter or margarine, melted

2 teaspoons Worcestershire sauce

½ teaspoon garlic powder

½ teaspoon chili powder

½ teaspoon onion powder

½ cup raisins

1. Preheat oven to 300 degrees.
2. In a large bowl, combine popcorn, cereal, croutons, pretzels and peanuts.
3. In a small bowl, whisk together butter, Worcestershire sauce, garlic powder, chili powder and onion powder. Pour over popcorn mixture; mix well.
4. Spread onto large cookie sheet and bake for 15 minutes; stir once or twice during baking.
5. Remove from oven and place in large bowl and mix in raisins.
6. Spread on cookie sheet and cool.

HINT: Mixing the raisins in after baking keeps them tender, chewy and plump! This recipe stores well in an airtight container.

Energy Boosters

MACHO NACHO POPCORN

I made a bowl of this and took it out to my friend's car when she was picking up her son from my house after a play date. Her daughter and girlfriend were in the car and proceeded to eat the whole bowl before my friend returned to the car with her son. The popcorn has a great nacho flavor. It is very easy to make and is much healthier than nacho chips.

Prep time: 5 min.	Microwave time: 3 min.	Quantity: 10 cups

½ teaspoon paprika

½ teaspoon cumin

⅛ teaspoon ground cayenne pepper

Pinch of sugar

¼ cup melted butter

1 package (3.5-ounce) microwave popcorn

½ cup Parmesan cheese, grated

1. In a small bowl, combine paprika, cumin, ground cayenne pepper and sugar; add melted butter and combine well.
2. Pop popcorn. Quickly toss with seasoned butter and Parmesan cheese ***immediately after popping!***
3. Serve!

HINT: If you want a milder flavor, use two packages of popcorn.

ZESTY POPCORN

Another popcorn recipe with great Italian flavor.

| Prep time: 2 min. | Microwave time: 3 min. | Quantity: 12 cups |

¼ cup butter or margarine, melted

1 envelope dry Italian salad dressing mix (Good Seasons® make a nice one)

2 packages (3.5-ounce each) microwave popcorn

1. In a small microwaveable bowl, combine melted butter with salad dressing mix; microwave 10-20 seconds.
2. Pop the popcorn and toss into large bowl with the above seasoning mixture.
3. Toss until well combined and serve.

HINT: Make sure the popcorn is hot when tossed with seasoning mixture.

POPCORN SALLY

This lightly seasoned snack is a recipe from my good friend Sally Dishaw.

| Prep time: 5 min. | Microwave time: 3 min. | Quantity: a great bowl of popcorn |

1 package (3.5-ounce) microwave popcorn

¼ cup butter or margarine, melted

¼ teaspoon garlic powder

¼ teaspoon onion powder

¼ cup Parmesan cheese, grated

⅛ teaspoon salt

1. In a small microwaveable bowl, combine melted butter, garlic powder, onion powder and cheese; microwave for 30 seconds.
2. Place hot popped popcorn in bowl and drizzle with above seasonings *immediately;* toss well.
3. Serve.

HOT SOCCER JUICE

Great for watching games on cold Saturday mornings.

| Prep time: 2 min. | Cook time: 10 min. | Quantity: 4 cups |

2 cups cranberry juice

2 cups pineapple juice

1 cinnamon stick

1. Place all three ingredients in medium saucepan and heat on low until hot and steaming, about 10 minutes (the longer the simmer the better the flavor).
2. Remove cinnamon stick and pour into thermos or mugs.
3. Serve hot.

SPICED TEA

You can remember your childhood when you think of summer and all of the fun things you did; whether it was swimming all day or playing baseball in the park with the neighborhood kids. I grew up in a big city and pools were not a common source of entertainment. The school playground, riding bikes, and frying eggs on sidewalks on very hot days were our pastimes. I have always loved to experiment with foods and this is one of the first recipes I ever made. It brings back summertime memories. Every time I make this spiced tea, I think of sitting on the back porch with my older sister, late in the afternoon, sipping this tea and playing with our dolls. What fond memories—many times I wish I could be there again.

Prep time: 5 min.	Cook time: none	Quantity: 5 cups

⅔ cup instant ice tea, unsweetened

2 cups sugar

2 cups Tang® orange flavored powdered drink mix

2 packages (.14-ounce each) Kool-Aid® unsweetened soft drink mix, lemonade flavor

2 teaspoons cinnamon

1 teaspoon cloves

1. Combine all ingredients; mix well. Keep in pantry in tightly sealed container.
2. Measure 1 heaping tablespoon spiced tea mix per 8-ounce glass of cold water.

HINT: Keeps 3 months (the whole summer!) in an airtight container.

FRUIT STICKS

Kids love the old standby fruit served in a new and unique way. Great for snacks or to take to a game.

Prep time: 10 min.   Cook time: none   Quantity: any quantity

1 large banana, sliced

1 large apple, sliced

1 watermelon, cubed

1 cantaloupe, cubed

1. Slice any of your favorite fruits and slide them on kabob sticks.
2. Dip bananas and apples in lemon juice before skewering, to keep from browning, if you are serving them later in the day.

HINT: Use any of your favorite fruits. Add a gumdrop or marshmallow on the ends to keep fruit from falling off or shifting.

2000 NUTS 'N BOLTS

This is a new and easier way of making an old-fashioned snack favorite. My friend, Lauren Zaworski, knows how lousy I am at making this snack in the oven. I always burn it. The microwave was the easy solution, but my daughter is still convinced that Mrs. Zaworski's is the best.

| Prep time: 5 min. | Microwave time: 8 min. | Quantity: A huge bowl! |

2 cups of each: Rice Chex®, Wheat Chex®, Corn Chex®, Cheerios®, salted peanuts and tiny pretzels

½ **cup margarine, melted**

¼ **cup Worcestershire sauce**

½ **teaspoon garlic powder**

½ **teaspoon onion powder**

1. Place all the cereals, peanuts and pretzels in large microwaveable bowl.
2. In a small bowl, combine melted margarine, Worcestershire sauce, garlic powder and onion powder until well mixed.
3. Pour seasoning mixture over cereal in large bowl; toss well.
4. Place in microwave and cook on High for 6-8 minutes; stir well every 2 minutes.
5. Cool on paper towels and serve or store in airtight container.

HINT: Tested in an 800-watt microwave. Times may vary based on wattage of microwave.

EASY PIZZA

Great dish to whip together—this pizza is always a favorite with the kids. You can even make it ahead of time, and then store in the refrigerator up to 8 hours. I have brought this to many functions as an appetizer and it is always the first thing to disappear!

Prep time: 5 min.	Bake time: 400°/13 min.	Quantity: 6 servings

1 container (10-ounce) refrigerated buttermilk biscuits

1½ tablespoons olive oil

2 teaspoons Italian seasoning

½ teaspoon garlic salt

½ large green pepper, chopped

½ large red pepper, chopped

½ small onion, chopped

1 cup mozzarella cheese, grated

1. Preheat oven to 400 degrees.
2. In the middle of a 12-inch pizza pan, arrange biscuits in a flat circle with the edges of each biscuit just touching. Press the biscuits down with fingers making them about ½-inch thick.
3. Brush biscuits with olive oil; sprinkle rest of ingredients on top of biscuits in order given.
4. Bake for 13-15 minutes or until edges are golden brown.
5. Serve.

HINT: Let the kids add their own toppings—fresh tomato, fresh herbs, diced ham, pepperoni, etc... If you do not have a pizza pan, use a large cookie sheet.

MINI PIZZA DOT SANDWICHES

An olive lover's snack. The kids can put this together with just a little of your help. Mini pizza dot sandwiches can also work as a quick dinner with a salad and some fresh fruit slices.

Prep time: 5 min.	Broil time: 1-2 min.	Quantity: 12 rounds

6 whole English muffins, halved

1 can (15-ounce) pizza sauce

2 cups mozzarella cheese, grated

1 can (6-ounce) pitted black olives, drained

1. Place muffin halves on a cookie sheet and spread pizza sauce over top; sprinkle with mozzarella cheese.
2. Slice the olives with a butter knife and place on top of cheese.
3. Broil for 1-2 minutes or until cheese melts and bubbles.
4. Cool slightly and serve.

Energy Boosters

QUICK COCOA MUFFIN CAKES

Rich cocoa taste with a firm texture. Handy for snacks at home, in the car or after a game.

| Prep time: 8 min. | Bake time: 375°/16 min. | Quantity: 1 dozen muffins |

1½ cups all-purpose flour

¾ cup brown sugar

¼ cup cocoa

1 teaspoon baking soda

½ teaspoon salt

1 cup water

¼ cup vegetable oil

1 tablespoon white vinegar

1 teaspoon vanilla

1. Preheat oven to 375 degrees.
2. Sift together flour, brown sugar, cocoa, baking soda and salt in medium bowl; add water, oil, vinegar and vanilla.
3. Beat with whisk or spoon just until batter is smooth and well blended; fill 12 paper lined muffin tins ⅔ full.
4. Bake 16-18 minutes or until wooden pick inserted in center comes out clean.
5. Cool in muffin tin for 10 minutes and then remove from pan and cool on wire rack.

HINT: Frosting is optional.

BLUEBERRY WHEAT MUFFINS

Not too sweet and very satisfying. Great to start the day, put in lunch boxes, after school snack, quick snack before game, quick snack after game, etc.... Get the picture?

Prep time: 10 min.   Bake time: 400°/20 min.   Quantity: 12 muffins

¾ cup all-purpose flour

¾ cup whole-wheat flour

½ cup brown sugar

1½ teaspoons baking powder

½ teaspoon salt

1¼ cups blueberries, frozen

1 large egg

½ cup milk

½ cup butter or margarine, melted

1. Preheat oven to 400 degrees.
2. In a large bowl, whisk white and whole-wheat flour, brown sugar, baking powder and salt; toss in blueberries to coat.
3. In a medium bowl, beat together egg, milk and butter; pour into dry ingredients; stir just until combined.
4. Fill paper lined muffin tins. Bake for 20 minutes.

HINT: These muffins freeze well.

REDEYE MUFFINS

Simple to put together and a perfect combination of tart and sweet.

| Prep time: 10 min. | Bake time: 350°/25 min. | Quantity: 18 muffins |

2 cups all-purpose flour

1 cup sugar

1½ teaspoons baking powder

½ teaspoon baking soda

½ teaspoon nutmeg

1 teaspoon cinnamon

½ teaspoon ginger

½ cup butter or margarine, melted

¾ cup orange juice

2 teaspoons vanilla

2 large eggs

1½ cups cranberries, fresh or frozen

1 cup chopped nuts, optional

1. Preheat oven to 350 degrees.
2. In a large bowl, whisk the first seven ingredients; add the butter. Mix with a fork until coarse crumbs.
3. In a small bowl, whisk the orange juice, vanilla and eggs; add to dry ingredients and stir just until moist, about 30 seconds. The batter will look slightly lumpy.
4. Gently fold in cranberries and nuts.
5. Spoon into paper lined muffin tins filling at least ¾ full.
6. Place muffins in oven immediately and bake for 25 minutes or until golden brown.

HINT: Frozen raspberries or blueberries can be used in place of cranberries. Just toss the berries with one tablespoon of flour before folding into batter. These muffins freeze well.

MUFFINS MADE EASY

Great tasting muffins cannot get much easier than this. The <u>key</u> is to just moisten the batter when you combine the wet ingredients with dry—do not beat!

Prep time: 10 min.	Bake time: 350°/20 min.	Quantity: 1 dozen

2 large eggs

½ cup sugar

¾ cup vegetable oil

3 tablespoons lemon juice

1 teaspoon grated lemon peel

1¼ cups all-purpose flour

1 teaspoon baking soda

¼ teaspoon salt

1 cup frozen blueberries

1. Preheat oven to 350 degrees.
2. In a large bowl, combine eggs, sugar and vegetable oil; whisk by hand for 2 minutes (this is the hardest part!). Stir lemon juice and grated lemon peel into beaten egg mixture.
3. In a small bowl, combine flour, baking soda and salt; whisk.
4. Sprinkle dry ingredients on top of wet ingredients; mix with wooden spoon just until combined.
5. Toss the frozen blueberries with 1 tablespoon of flour and place in batter; give a stroke or two just to mix in.
6. Pour into paper-lined muffin tins and bake for 20-22 minutes.

VARIATIONS: Add ½ teaspoon of nutmeg and ginger to the flour and proceed as directed. You can use fresh blueberries in place of frozen. These muffins freeze well.

WHOLE GRAIN MASTER MIX

This is my original pancake mix and the basis for the following three recipes. This mix can be prepared in advance and stored at room temperature. It keeps well for up to two months. Measure like you would flour. This is very handy when you need to make biscuits, pancakes, waffles, or muffins in a snap.

| Prep time: 10 min. | Cook time: none | Quantity: approx. 7 cups |

2 cups all-purpose flour

2 cups whole-wheat flour

¾ cup nonfat dry milk powder

½ cup quick oats

½ cup cornmeal

2 tablespoons baking powder

2 tablespoons sugar

1 teaspoon salt

½ cup vegetable oil

1. Combine all above ingredients except the oil.
2. Cut oil in with pastry blender until coarse cornmeal consistency.
3. Store in covered container at room temperature up to 2 months.

MASTER MIX BISCUITS

Rich and hearty—perfect for beef and gravy.

| Prep time: 5 min. | Bake time: 400°/10 min. | Quantity: 15-20 biscuits |

3 cups master mix (not packed)

⅔ cup water, add more if needed

1. Preheat oven to 400 degrees.
2. Combine above ingredients and knead 10 times.
3. Roll out dough until ½-inch thick on lightly floured surface; cut with 2-inch diameter cutter*.
4. Bake on un-greased baking sheet.

*Can be a 2-inch diameter glass, cookie cutter or metal biscuit cutter. Dip cutter in flour to keep dough from sticking.

MASTER MIX PANCAKES/WAFFLES

Hearty mix that holds up well with any kind of syrup or jam!

Prep time: 2 min.   Griddle time: 3 min.   Quantity: 18 cakes or 6 waffles

3 cups master mix (not packed)

1½ cups water

1 egg

1. Mix until blended.
2. Pour onto hot griddle or waffle iron and cook until golden brown.

MASTER MIX MUFFINS

Perfect any time!

Prep time: 5 min.   Cook time: 400°/18 min.   Quantity: 12 muffins

3 cups master mix (not packed)

2 tablespoons sugar

1 cup water

1 egg, beaten

½ cup dried fruit, chopped nuts or frozen blueberries or raspberries

1. Preheat oven to 400 degrees.

2. Spray muffin tin with non-stick cooking spray.

3. In a large mixing bowl combine ingredients; stir until ingredients are barely moistened.

4. Fill muffin tins ⅔ full and bake for 18 minutes.

HINT: Sprinkle a little cinnamon-sugar over the tops of muffins before baking.

WARM-UPS

Soup, salads, sandwiches and miscellaneous goodies that are great for lunch or dinner—convenience and nutrition were in mind when creating these recipes. Like the recipes in the other chapters, a lot of the ingredients are already in your pantry or refrigerator.

Soup, salad and sandwiches warm the soul and satisfy that craving for the mid-day meal. The soups in this chapter have wonderful flavor. The salad choices can satisfy all the family needs: potluck dinners, group dinners or quick eating on the run!

You will also find some great sandwiches and salads in the **15 MINUTE DISHES** chapter!!

Warm Ups

BLT SOUP

This is something my kids just love. It tastes just like a BLT sandwich.

Prep time: 10 min.   Cook time: 15 min.   Quantity: 4-6 servings

8 slices bacon, cut into 2-inch pieces

1 medium onion, chopped

1-2 stalks celery, chopped

3 cups beef broth

1 can (14.5-ounce) diced tomatoes

1 tablespoon Worcestershire sauce

¼ - ½ teaspoon garlic powder

1 teaspoon parsley

½ teaspoon thyme

½ teaspoon pepper

Dash of hot sauce (optional)

2 cups lettuce, shredded

Seasoned croutons

1. In a large saucepan, cook bacon until crisp.
2. Remove bacon from pan and discard drippings except for 2 tablespoons.
3. Sauté onion and celery in drippings until soft, stirring frequently, about 8 minutes.
4. Add broth, tomatoes, Worcestershire sauce, garlic powder, parsley, thyme, pepper and hot sauce; bring to a boil. Reduce heat and simmer for 15-20 minutes.
5. Serve hot in bowls, topping soup with shredded lettuce, reserved bacon and croutons.

DELIGHTFUL CHICKEN SOUP

Linda Flint tested this recipe (and many others!) and found it delightful because of the ease of preparation and the fresh flavors. Thanks, Linda, for feeding your family all the test recipes!

Prep time: 5 min.   Cook time: 15 min.   Quantity: 4-6 servings

7 cups chicken broth

2 large carrots, grated or finely chopped

2-3 stalks of celery, chopped

1 small onion, chopped

2 cans (15-ounce each) great northern beans, drained

½ teaspoon black pepper

1 cup washed fresh spinach leaves, chopped*

1. In a large pot over medium-high heat, combine broth, carrots, celery and onion; bring to a boil.
2. Lower heat and simmer until celery is tender, about 10 minutes; add beans, pepper, and spinach.
3. Simmer for 2 minutes until spinach is bright green.
4. Serve hot.

HINT: Sprinkle with Parmesan cheese and croutons when serving. Serve with French bread and sliced fruit.

*This dish really benefits from the fresh spinach but if in a rush use a 10-ounce package of frozen chopped spinach.

TEXAS CORN CHOWDER

A great dish that takes so little effort. If you can use a can opener, you can make this soup.

Prep time: 5 min.   Cook time: 5 min.   Quantity: 4-6 servings

1 can (15-ounce) whole kernel corn, drained

1 can (15-ounce) cream style corn

1 can (14.5-ounce) diced tomatoes with garlic and onions

1 can (15-ounce) black beans, rinsed and drained

½ cup chicken broth

1. Combine all the above ingredients in medium saucepan.
2. Simmer for 5 minutes and serve.

HINT: To add a little interest to the soup you may want to add cheddar cheese, fresh chopped green pepper or sour cream.

HIGH PROTEIN TOMATO SOUP

This recipe will supply kids with plenty of the calcium and protein needed for growing bodies.

Prep time: 3 min.   Microwave time: 5 min.   Quantity: 4 servings

1 can (10½-ounce) condensed tomato soup

1 soup can (10½-ounce) **_whole_** milk

½ cup grated cheddar cheese

1. In a medium microwaveable bowl, combine soup, milk and cheese; heat through.
2. Stir occasionally until cheese melts.
3. Serve immediately.

HINT: Serve with sliced cucumbers and saltine crackers, or toasted garlic bread. Leftover rice in the soup works well, too!

Lyn and Paula Scrimger, my neighbors, were so generous with their time when testing recipes for the cookbook. They have two incredible daughters who are now grown and are outstanding individuals (thanks to Lyn and Paula). My husband and I watched them the past seven years zooming in and out of the drive going to sporting events, music recitals, band concerts, track meets, soccer tournaments, honors banquets and on and on and on... I now understand what they lived by—loving their children, spending time with their children, making sure there was enough gas in the car and food in the fridge!

MIDWESTERN CORN CHOWDER

In the late fall, people from the Midwest describe the weather as sharp, brisk, biting, crisp, or darn right cold. This calls for a hot bowl of hearty soup. This soup is quick, easy and seals the essence of that crisp day in November.

Prep time: 15 min.	Cook time: 15 min.	Quantity: 4-6 servings

2 tablespoons vegetable oil

3 cups good quality ham, cubed

1 medium onion, finely chopped

1 stalk of celery, finely chopped

4 cups chicken broth

2 large potatoes, diced

1 bay leaf

1 teaspoon salt

1½ cups **whole** milk

2½ tablespoons all-purpose flour

1 can (15-ounce) whole kernel corn, drained

2 cups milk

1. In a large pot, warm oil over medium-high heat; sauté ham, onion and celery for 5 minutes.
2. Add broth, potatoes, bay leaf and salt to pot; bring to a simmer. When potatoes are barely tender, about 8 minutes, remove from heat.
3. In a small bowl, combine 1½ cups milk with flour; whisk; add to large pot. Simmer over medium-low heat until thickened, about 15 minutes.
4. Add corn and 2 cups of milk. Heat through and serve.

HINT: Can be made up to two days in advance. Just re-heat and serve.

PEANUT SOUP

Thick and rich with a pleasant peanut taste. This recipe is delicious.

Prep time: 10 min.   Cook time: 10 min.   Quantity: 4-6 servings

4 cups chicken broth

1 can (14.25-ounce) stewed tomatoes

2-3 carrots, chopped

2 bunches green onions, chopped

1 cup peanut butter

1 cup milk

¼ cup instant mashed potato flakes

1. In a large saucepan, combine broth, tomatoes, carrots and green onions; bring to a boil.
2. Reduce heat to medium-low; simmer until carrots are tender, about 5 minutes.
3. Stir in peanut butter until well blended.
4. Add milk and potato flakes; simmer 2 minutes.
5. Serve.

HINT: Serve with French bread and salad. "Great if made in advance and re-heated—the flavors have time to 'marry'. " —Barb Mansfield

SALAD FOR SOCCER PARENTS

A wonderful crisp salad full of flavor!

| Prep time: 5 min. | Marinate time: 30 min. | Quantity: 6-8 servings |

¾ cup extra virgin olive oil

¼ cup rice vinegar

½ cup dried apricots, cut in quarters

2 bags (16-ounce each) pre-made salad

3 ounces bleu cheese, crumbled

½ cup chopped walnuts

1 cup croutons, plain or seasoned

1. In a small bowl, combine oil and vinegar; whisk. Add apricots and marinate for 30 minutes.
2. Empty pre-made salad in a large salad bowl; sprinkle with cheese and walnuts.
3. Pour marinade over all; toss; sprinkle croutons.
4. Serve.

NOTE: Kitchen shears cut dried fruit easily to make smaller pieces.

Warm-Ups

CUCUMBER TOMATO RED ONION SALAD

Nothing can be better than a fresh salad on a hot summer evening. This is just the ticket—quick, easy and tasty!

| Prep time: 5 min. | Marinate time: 30 min. | Cook time: none | Quantity: 6-8 servings |

3 large cucumbers, peeled

4 pints cherry tomatoes, halved

¼ small red onion, chopped

6 tablespoons olive oil

¼ cup **fresh lemon juice**

½ teaspoon salt

⅛ teaspoon pepper

¼ teaspoon red pepper flakes

1. Cut cucumber in half lengthwise, scoop out and discard seeds; cut into ½-inch pieces.
2. In a small bowl, combine oil, lemon juice, salt, pepper and red pepper; whisk.
3. In a large bowl, combine cucumber, tomato and red onion; pour on dressing; toss.
4. Let stand at room temperature for half an hour to 4 hours before serving.

HINT: A little Feta cheese on top adds a lot of flavor!

MANDARIN SALAD

This is not the quickest salad in the West, but I believe it's the tastiest! The sugared almonds make this salad—they add crunch, texture and flavor!

Prep time: 15 min.   Cook time: 3 min.   Quantity: 4-6 servings

Salad

½ cup sliced almonds

1 bag (16-ounce) pre-made salad

2 whole green onions, chopped

Salt and pepper

3 tablespoons sugar

2 stalks celery, chopped

1 can (11-ounce) mandarin oranges, drained

1. In a small skillet over medium-high heat, warm almonds and sugar, stirring constantly until almonds are coated and sugar has dissolved (being careful not to let burn), about 3-5 minutes. Cool on paper towels and store in airtight container up to one week before using.

2. When ready to serve, arrange pre-made salad, celery and green onions in a large salad bowl; toss.

3. Add oranges, sugared almonds and dressing; toss. Salt and pepper to taste; serve.

Dressing

½ teaspoon salt

¼ cup vegetable oil

2 tablespoons sugar

2 tablespoons vinegar (preferably red wine vinegar)

⅛ teaspoon pepper

1 tablespoon fresh parsley, chopped

A squirt or two of hot sauce

1. Combine all ingredients in small bowl with airtight lid. Shake well and store in refrigerator up to one week. Shake well before pouring onto salad.

A note to a special friend: Thank you Lauren, for sharing this wonderful recipe and many others!

MAKE YOUR OWN ANTIPASTO PASTA

This pasta dish is like a deli counter. Some people like ham and some people like salami. You can pick and choose your own ingredients.

Prep time: 5 min.   Cook time: 20 min.   Quantity: 4-6 servings

1 pound pasta, your choice

Anything you may want to chop up for an antipasto salad, or use examples given below:

1 jar (6-ounce) marinated artichoke hearts, quartered

1 jar (12-ounce) roasted red peppers, sliced

⅓ pound salami, cut up

⅓ pound ham, cut up

¼ red onion, chopped

1 large tomato, chopped

Broccoli flowerets

¼ pound provolone cheese, cubed or grated

A home-made, zesty Italian, Caesar or Greek dressing

1. While boiling pasta, prepare all the above ingredients and toss in medium bowl.
2. Drain pasta and toss with the above ingredients; drizzle with dressing.
3. Serve hot, warm or cold!

HINT: Remember that most of your preparation can be done while the pasta is cooking.

INFAMOUS UNTOSSED SALAD

If you are not aware of this type of salad you have to try this recipe. For those who are aware of this recipe I think my version is the best, of course! This recipe is great when you have a crowd of people over for the weekend. You can make it in advance and serve it all weekend. It is truly a winner!

| Prep time: 15 min. | Refrigerate: overnight | Cook time: none | Quantity: 8-10 servings |

1 large head of lettuce, shredded

2 bunches green onions, chopped (or ½ red onion, chopped)

1 bag (10-ounce) frozen peas, thawed

3 tablespoons bacon (bacon pieces in a jar work great!)

5 hard boiled eggs, peeled and chopped

1 cup Miracle Whip®

2 tablespoons sugar

1 cup cheddar or Swiss cheese

1. In a 9x13-inch glass casserole dish, layer the first five ingredients; spread on Miracle Whip®.
2. Sprinkle sugar and cheese over top; cover and refrigerate overnight or up to 2-3 days.
3. Serve at your convenience.

GREEK VEGGIE SALAD

Willie Busch is a great friend of mine who is the most incredible dancer I have ever met. Most of her large family is grown and married now, but she knows what it is like to have a family on the run. She helped test recipes for this book and had many helpful comments and additions and I thank her. She loved this salad and suggested serving this with grilled chicken on a summer evening.

Prep time: 8 min.	Cook time: none	Quantity: 4-6 servings

2-3 medium cucumbers, diced (peeling and seeding optional)

1 container (8-ounce) plain yogurt

1 large garlic clove, crushed*

1½ teaspoons dill

2 teaspoons vinegar (white wine or cider works well)

¾ teaspoon salt

Pepper to taste

1. In a small bowl, combine all the above ingredients; mix well.
2. Cover and chill until ready to serve.

*Use chopped or minced ready to use garlic in the jar for convenience.

GREEN NUGGET SALAD

Super quick and easy, this salad is perfect for a potluck or summer side dish. The water chestnuts give this dish a pleasant crunch!

| Prep time: 5 min. | Chill time: 10 min. | Quantity: 4-6 servings |

½ cup sour cream

3 tablespoons vinegar, red wine or cider vinegar

1 tablespoon milk

2 teaspoons sugar

½ teaspoon salt

¼ teaspoon garlic powder

1 package (10-ounce) frozen peas, thawed

1 can (8-ounce) sliced water chestnuts, drained

1 bunch green onions, thinly sliced

⅓ cup cooked bacon bits

1. In a small bowl, combine sour cream, vinegar, milk, sugar, salt and garlic powder; whisk. Chill 10 minutes before continuing.
2. Pat the peas dry with a paper towel; combine in a large bowl with water chestnuts, green onions and bacon.
3. Toss with dressing. Serve.

HINT: Adding ½ cup dry roasted peanuts or cashews makes a delightful change. Can be prepared and refrigerated up to two days in advance.

Warm-Ups

THE EASIEST COLE SLAW

Cole slaw is easy to buy, but the store bought kind never tastes fresh. This recipe is so easy to make and lasts a good week in the fridge. You will be amazed at how tasty and easy this fresh recipe is.

| Prep time: 10 min. | Cook time: none | Quantity: 6-8 servings |

1 bag (16-ounce) prepackaged Cole-slaw salad mix

1 small onion, thinly sliced

½ cup mayonnaise

¼ cup sour cream

2 tablespoons vinegar

2 teaspoons Dijon mustard

¼ teaspoon sugar

¼ teaspoon salt

Pepper to taste

2 tablespoons caraway seeds (optional)

1. In a large bowl, toss slaw mix with onions.
2. In a small bowl, combine mayonnaise, sour cream, vinegar, Dijon mustard, sugar and salt; whisk. Pour over slaw mix.
3. Toss slaw dressing with slaw and onion mixture; season with pepper and caraway seeds.
4. Refrigerate and serve when needed.

Warm-Ups

CHICKEN AND CHERRY SALAD

Michigan dried cherries are outstanding and are now available all across the United States. This recipe is perfect to bring in a cooler and stuff in pitas between tournament games. Some cool raspberry iced tea, celery and carrot sticks and off you go!

Prep time: 15 min.	Cook time: none	Quantity: 4 servings

½ cup dried tart cherries

2 **_cooked_** boneless, skinless chicken breast halves, cubed

2 stalks celery, finely chopped

1 large Granny Smith apple, finely chopped

½ cup walnuts, chopped

1 cup mayonnaise

2 tablespoons fresh parsley, finely chopped

1. In a small bowl combine cherries with ¼ cup boiling water. Let stand for 5 minutes or until cherries have plumped up; drain and pat dry.
2. In a medium bowl, combine cherries, chicken, celery, apple, walnuts, mayonnaise and parsley; mix well. Add salt and pepper to taste.
3. Chill before serving.

HINT: This can be served on a bed of lettuce or stuffed in pita with leaf lettuce. The salad keeps well in the refrigerator for up to 3 days.

CHICKEN SALAD LISA

My daughter, Lisa, will eat anything as long as it has ranch dressing in it or on it. She created this recipe one day in the kitchen and loves to make it with leftover rotisserie chicken.

| Prep time: 5 min. | Cook time: none | Quantity: 4-6 servings |

2-3 **_cooked_** chicken breasts halves, cubed

2 stalks celery, chopped

1 can (20-ounce) pineapple chunks in natural juice, drained (reserve ¼ cup of juice)

1 package (1-ounce) ranch salad dressing mix

½ cup mayonnaise

1. In a medium bowl, combine chicken, celery and pineapple chunks.
2. In a smaller bowl, combine dressing mix, mayonnaise and ¼ cup of reserved pineapple juice; mix well. Pour over chicken; mix well.
3. Serve now or refrigerate and serve later.

HINT: Optional additions to salad could be chopped nuts and/or sliced apples. Serve on hard rolls or pita pockets with sliced veggies or on a bed of greens with sliced fruit on the side.

Warm-Ups

CHICKEN SALAD BARBEQUE

Creamy and spicy—this is a delicious recipe for any kind of cooked chicken. I have made this a million times with baked, roasted, or barbecued chicken and it tastes different every time. My family never knows if it's leftover or made for the occasion. It is one of my little secrets.

Prep time: 10 min.   Cook time: none   Quantity: 4-6 servings

2 **_cooked_** whole chickens; grilled, barbecued, rotisserie, etc.

⅓ cup spicy barbecue sauce

⅓ cup mayonnaise

1-2 jalapeño peppers, chopped fine (optional)

1 bunch green onion, chopped

1 red or green pepper, chopped

Salt and pepper, to taste

1. Remove chicken meat from bone; chop into small cubes.
2. Place chicken with all other ingredients in a large bowl; mix well. Season with salt and pepper.
3. Serve on pita with leaf lettuce or on salad greens.

SEVEN LAYER CHICKEN SALAD

Excellent for a cookout!

| Prep time: 10 min. | Cook time: none | Quantity: 4-6 servings |

1 head clean romaine lettuce, broken up

1 package (3-ounce) Ramen® noodle soup mix, any flavor

2 cups cooked chicken, diced

1 can (15-ounce) whole kernel corn, drained

1 large tomato, chopped

4 green onions, sliced

½ cup chopped walnuts, pecans or dry roasted peanuts

Salad dressing of your choice

1. Place lettuce in a large serving bowl.
2. Discard seasoning packet from noodles and crush noodles; place on top of lettuce.
3. Layer remaining ingredients listed above in order given; refrigerate up to one day in advance.
4. When ready to serve, add your favorite salad dressing.

HINT: A light vinaigrette dressing or ranch dressing would be perfect for this salad.

QUICK ORIENTAL CHICKEN SALAD

Brian Kendall's mom, Cindy, tested this salad for the cookbook. Brian loves this salad so much that he makes a point, every time he sees me, of letting me know how much he enjoys the light and crunchy texture of it!

Prep time: 5 min.	Cook time: none	Quantity: 6-8 servings

1 bag (16-ounce) tortilla chips, slightly broken

1 large head of lettuce, torn

4 cups **cooked** chicken, shredded or diced (canned chicken works too!)

1-2 bunches green onions, chopped

2 tablespoons sesame seeds, toasted*

½ cup vegetable oil

¼ cup vinegar (rice or cider)

3 tablespoons sugar

1 tablespoon sesame oil

½ teaspoon salt

½ teaspoon black pepper

1. In the bottom of a large bowl, layer the chips, lettuce, chicken, onions and sesame seeds.
2. In a small airtight container, combine vegetable oil, vinegar, sugar, sesame oil, salt and pepper; cover and shake well.
3. Pour over salad and toss gently and thoroughly.
4. Serve immediately.

*Place sesame seeds in small frying pan over medium heat for 2-3 minutes or until seeds are golden; remove from heat immediately. Keep a **very** close eye on them.*

HINT: Put a dash of soy sauce or ginger powder into the dressing for a new and interesting taste.

Variations

Shredded cooked pork instead of chicken

Unsalted tortilla chips for lower sodium content

Fresh spinach and romaine instead of head lettuce

MEXICAN BEEF SALAD

This is a fresher and lighter version of a typical Mexican salad. Serve this with crumbled taco chips and salsa on top for a nice crunchy change.

| Prep time: 10 min. | Cook time: none | Quantity: 4-6 servings |

1 pound ground beef

1 small onion, chopped

1 tablespoon chili powder

$\frac{1}{2}$ teaspoon salt

$\frac{1}{4}$ teaspoon pepper

1 head lettuce, chopped

2 large tomatoes, diced

$\frac{1}{2}$ cup Italian salad dressing

$\frac{1}{2}$-1 cup cheddar cheese, grated

6 large tortilla baskets, store bought (optional)

1. In a medium skillet over medium heat, cook beef and onion until brown.
2. Remove pan from heat; drain off fat. Add chili powder, salt and pepper; stir well. Cool slightly.
3. In a large serving bowl, combine lettuce and tomato. Add seasoned beef, salad dressing and cheese; toss well.
4. Serve in bowls, tortilla basket, or taco shells.

HINT: You can use ground turkey in place of beef. Seasoned and cooked meat can be made in advance and stored in refrigerator for up to 2 days or frozen for up to 2 months.

DRESSED UP TUNA

This is a great recipe for the tuna lover who ran out of mayo. The curry makes this dish very unique (thanks for the tip, Sally*). The tuna salad can be made a day in advance and refrigerated until ready to stuff in pitas.

Prep time: 5 min.	Cook time: none	Quantity: 4 half pitas

1 can (6-ounce) tuna, drained and flaked

⅓ -½ cup plain yogurt

1 stalk celery, chopped in small pieces

½ teaspoon dill weed

⅛ teaspoon garlic powder

¼+ teaspoon curry powder

¼ teaspoon salt

Pepper to taste

2 pita bread, halved

8 lettuce leaves

Tomato slices

1. In a medium bowl, combine tuna, yogurt, celery, dill weed, garlic powder, curry powder, salt and pepper.
2. Line pita pockets with lettuce leaves and tomato so the tuna does not saturate the bread; spoon the tuna into the four pockets.
3. Eat immediately or wrap and refrigerate until the next day.

*I can always count on my friend, Sally Dishaw, to give me the perfect ingredient to make a dish really sing!

COUNTRY RANCH POTATO SALAD

Kids will love this potato salad.

Prep time: 10 min.   Cook time: 20 min.   Quantity: 12-16 servings

10-12 medium russet potatoes, cubed (peeling optional)

3 stalks celery, chopped

½ red onion, finely chopped

1 package (1-ounce) ranch salad dressing mix

1 cup mayonnaise

1 tablespoon dehydrated onions

½ tablespoon dried dill

2 teaspoons vinegar, any kind

½ cup water

Salt and pepper to taste

1. Boil potatoes in a large pot of water. When potatoes are barely fork tender, drain and rinse in cold water.
2. In a large bowl, combine potatoes, celery and onions.
3. In a small bowl, combine dressing mix, mayonnaise, dehydrated onions, dill, vinegar and water; mix well. Pour dressing over potatoes and toss until well coated.
4. Chill and serve.

HINT: Pre-packaged boiled potatoes will do in a pinch.

TEXAS T-BALL POTATO SALAD

Crunchy and rich—a great dish to bring to a picnic.

Prep time: 5 min.   Cook time: 15 min.   Quantity: 6-8 servings

5-6 large russet potatoes (peeling is optional)

½-1 cup Miracle Whip® (regular or light)

2 teaspoons chili powder

1 teaspoon onion powder

1 can (15-ounce) whole kernel corn, drained

1 can (4-ounce) green chilies, chopped

1 large stalk celery, chopped

1 red sweet pepper, chopped

1. Cut potatoes into large cubes and boil until fork tender, about 15 minutes; drain; cool slightly.
2. In a large bowl, whisk dressing, chili powder and onion powder together.
3. Add cooked potatoes and remaining ingredients to dressing; toss well. Salt and pepper to taste.
4. Serve warm or refrigerate up to 1 week.

HINT: You can use 5-6 cups of small red potatoes in place of the russets for a different texture and taste.

Warm-Ups

SPRING PRACTICE SALAD

This is a great side dish to bring to your mother-in-law's house for any holiday. You know she is the more experienced cook, but she will be quite impressed with this dish and only you will know how easy it was. It has a creamy texture and the mild flavors blend nicely.

| Prep time: 10 min. | Cook time: 8 min. | Quantity: 4-6 servings |

2 cups cooked rice (instant rice works well), cooled slightly

1 can (15-ounce) mandarin oranges, drained

¼ cup plain yogurt

¼ cup mayonnaise

1-2 teaspoons lemon juice

1 teaspoon honey

¼ cup toasted sliced almonds*

⅓ cup toasted coconut*

Salt and pepper

1. Combine all ingredients together; salt and pepper to taste.
2. Chill and serve!

*HINT: To toast almonds, place in small, dry skillet over medium heat. Cook until just brown, about 3-5 minutes (watch carefully). Do the same procedure with coconut. Cool on paper towels.

VARIATIONS:

Add cooked chicken to create a main dish.

Use red grapes as an alternative to mandarin oranges.

Warm-Ups

FREE-THROW SALAD

Things can't get much easier than this! Sweet and satisfying.

Prep time: 5 min.	Chill time: 2 hrs.	Cook time: none	Quantity: 6-8 servings

1 pound cottage cheese

1 container (8-ounce) frozen whipped topping, thawed

1 can (20-ounce) crushed pineapple, drained

1 package (6-ounce) flavored gelatin, any flavor

1. Combine all ingredients well.
2. Chill and serve!

HINT: Lime gelatin is my favorite in this recipe.

PITA ANTIPASTO

Don't be concerned with the quantity of ingredients listed—this recipe is quick, easy, packed with flavor and crunch, and loaded with nutrition! You can't go wrong with this one.

Prep time: 15 min.	Cook time: 15 min.	Chill time: 2 hrs.	Quantity: 4-6 servings

2 cups Italian salad dressing, the zestier the better

¼ cup water

½ teaspoon dry mustard

3-4 carrots, peeled and sliced finely

½ head cauliflower, broken into small flowerets

¼ pound mushrooms, sliced

½ cup black olives, sliced

⅓ pound salami, cut-up

½ cup provolone cheese, diced

1 jar (2-ounce) pimento, drained and chopped

1 can (6-ounce) tuna, drained

6 pita rounds

1. In a medium saucepan, combine salad dressing, water and dry mustard; bring to a boil. Add carrots and cauliflower and boil gently until vegetables are tender but still crisp, about 10 minutes.

2. Remove vegetables with slotted spoon to a large bowl. Add mushrooms to boiling marinade and boil gently for 3 minutes. Remove mushrooms with slotted spoon to same bowl as carrots and cauliflower.

3. Discard all but ½ cup cooking liquid. Refrigerate the reserved half the cooking liquid to be used as a dressing.

4. Add olives, salami, cheese, pimento and tuna to vegetables; combine gently with spoon. Refrigerate vegetable mixture until well chilled.

5. Serve in pita drizzled with reserved dressing.

*My mother is an **outstanding** cook and has taught me more than I can ever list when it comes to working in the kitchen. She tested this and many other recipes for this book, offering great suggestions. I am very lucky to have worked beside her all these years in her Italian kitchen. Thanks, Mom!*

CHICKEN WRAPS

A taco inspired dish. A nice meal to make when you have an evening on the go....

> Prep time: 5 min.   Cook time: 15 min.   Quantity: 4-6 servings

1 tablespoon vegetable oil

2-3 boneless, skinless chicken breasts halves cut into thin strips

2 cups water

1 cup salsa

1 package (1¼-ounce) taco seasoning mix

2 cups *instant* rice, *uncooked*

8-12 tortillas

1. In a large skillet, warm oil over medium-high heat. Add chicken and sauté until cooked through, about 6-8 minutes.
2. Add water, salsa and seasoning mix to skillet; stir until combined; bring to a boil.
3. Stir in rice; reduce heat to low and cover. Cook for 5 minutes.
4. Serve in tortillas while still hot.

HINT: Serve with grated cheddar cheese, lettuce or tomato. You can use 1 pound of top sirloin steak cut into thin strips instead of chicken.

ITALIAN COUNTRY SANDWICH

*This is a **great** sandwich loaded with flavor. You can find focaccia (Italian flat bread) at most local bakeries and well stocked grocery stores. If you cannot find focaccia then you can substitute a thick crust pizza shell.*

Prep time: 5 min.	Bake time: 350°/20 min.	Quantity: 8-12 servings

2 - 8-inch focaccia (Italian flat bread)

1 container (8-ounce) seasoned cream cheese (garden vegetable works well!)

1 large tomato, thinly sliced

1 large green pepper, thinly sliced

6-8 slices pastrami, thinly sliced

6-8 slices salami, thinly sliced

2-4 thin slices red onion

8 slices provolone or mozzarella cheese (or 1 cup grated)

1. Preheat oven to 350 degrees.
2. Slice both breads in half **horizontally** and lie on two separate pieces of aluminum foil; spread bottom halves with cream cheese.
3. Layer tomato, green pepper, pastrami, salami, red onion and provolone cheese on top of cream cheese. Cover with other half of bread; wrap tightly in foil.
4. Bake 20–25 minutes or until hot.
5. Cut into squares or wedges depending on style of bread.

OPEN FACE BEEF SANDWICH

I couldn't get enough of open face roast beef sandwiches with mashed potatoes when I was a kid. This is an easy way of making that sandwich. To create one of those 'heart warming meals' combine this recipe with mashed potatoes, applesauce and a big glass of milk.

| Prep time: 5 min. | Cook time: 10 min. | Quantity: 2-3 servings |

¼ cup low sodium soy sauce

1 package (.87-ounce) brown gravy mix

1½ cups water

8 ounces sliced roast beef (premium quality deli meat)

Sliced French bread

1. In a medium skillet, combine soy sauce, gravy mix and 1½ cups of water.
2. Cook as directed on gravy package.
3. Add beef and heat until warm.
4. Serve over slices of French bread.

REUBEN LOAF

This was given to me by a good friend who moved to Texas. She always has a great recipe for any occasion.

| Prep time: 20 min. | Bake time: 400°/22 min. | Quantity: 4-6 servings |

1 loaf frozen bread dough, thawed

¼ cup Thousand Island dressing

6 ounces thinly sliced corned beef

¼-pound sliced Swiss cheese

6-8 ounces sauerkraut, drained well

1. Preheat oven to 400 degrees.
2. Roll bread dough out to a 14x10-inch rectangle. Place on a large greased baking sheet.
3. Spread dressing down middle third of dough; top with corned beef, Swiss cheese and sauerkraut.
4. Make cuts in dough from filling to dough edges at 1-inch intervals along sides of filling.
5. By alternating sides, fold strips at an angle across filling.
6. Let loaf rest for 15 minutes.
7. Bake for 22-24 minutes.
8. Cool slightly; slice and serve.

OPEN FACE PIZZA HOAGIES

This recipe has a tart zesty flavor that complements the pork. These are perfect for the kids when having a sleepover. Most of it can be done in advance.

Prep time: 10 min.   Marinate time: 2-24 hrs.   Bake time: 350°/10 min.   Quantity: 4-6 servings

6 (4-ounce each) boneless pork loin chops, cut into thin strips

½ cup Italian salad dressing

1 cup pizza sauce

1 cup mozzarella or provolone cheese, grated

4 hoagie buns

1. Preheat oven to 350 degrees.
2. Marinate pork strips in salad dressing 2-24 hours in refrigerator.
3. Warm skillet over medium-high heat. Pour meat and marinade into skillet and fry 6-8 minutes or until meat is slightly browned.
4. Slice hoagie buns length-wise and place on cookie sheet.
5. Spread pizza sauce evenly over bun. Place cooked pork strips on top of sauce and with sprinkle cheese.
6. Bake for 10 minutes and serve.

TUNA SANDWICH UNIQUE

A unique combination of fruit, nuts and seasoning. This is a great spread to make mid-week, in advance, when you know that Saturday will be one of those days when you have events back-to-back all day and you need to have lunch ready immediately.

Prep time: 5 min.	Cook time: none	Quantity: 4 servings

2 cans (6-ounce each) tuna, drained and flaked

¼ cup currants or chopped raisins

¼ cup walnuts or pecans, finely chopped

4 green onions, finely chopped

¾ cup mayonnaise

1 tablespoon curry powder

Salt and pepper to taste

1. In a medium bowl, combine all ingredients; mix well.
2. Store in refrigerator for up to 3 days.
3. Stuff in pita or spread on sandwich bread and always remember to add a big leaf of lettuce for some crunch!

15 MINUTE DISHES

Quick, easy, and ready to go! These dishes take 15
minutes or less to make and serve.

A hectic day means you need something easy and
quick for dinner. There are many selections to choose
from in this chapter to satisfy anyone's tastes. Remember
to check the WARM-UPS chapter for more quick meals
to prepare in under 15 minutes!

PINK RIVER BURGERS

The onion in this gives a nice crunch!

Prep time: 5 min.   Cook time: 10 min.   Quantity: 4 burgers

1 can (6-ounce) skinless, boneless salmon, drained

¼ cup breadcrumbs

¼ cup onion, finely chopped

2 tablespoons mayonnaise

1 large egg, beaten

1 teaspoon lemon juice

1 teaspoon parsley flakes

¼ teaspoon garlic salt

3 tablespoons vegetable oil

1. In a medium bowl, combine everything except vegetable oil; shape into 4 large patties.
2. In a large skillet, warm oil over medium-high heat. Add burgers to skillet and brown on both sides, about 5 minutes on each side.
3. Serve on buns with mustard, cocktail or tartar sauce.

COBB SALAD PITAS

I fell in love with the Cobb salad when I had my first real job out of college. I had enough money to actually go out to lunch once a week! The Cobb salad is still my favorite. The mixture of flavors work perfectly together. This recipe makes it easy to bring your Cobb salad with you when you're 'on the go'!

Prep time: 5 min.	Cook time: none	Quantity: 4 servings

1 cup mixed grated cheese, your choice

1 cup tomato, chopped

1 large avocado, diced

1 can (5-ounce) cooked chicken, drained and flaked

⅓ cup bacon bits

⅓ cup Italian dressing

1-2 cups grated lettuce

4 pitas, halved

1. In a medium bowl, combine cheese, tomato, avocado, chicken, bacon and dressing; mix well.
2. Toss in grated lettuce.
3. Open pita pockets and fill with salad mixture.
4. Serve.

HINT: Do step one in advance, possibly in the morning and refrigerate; combining with lettuce before serving!

VEGGIE MIX SALAD

A favorite main dish salad. The creamy dressing compliments the flavors of the broccoli and cauliflower. Quick and easy to eat by itself or on a bed of lettuce.

Prep time: 15 min.	Marinate: overnight	Cook time: none	Quantity: 10 servings

2 bunches broccoli florets

1 head cauliflower

6 large hard-boiled eggs

1 medium onion, chopped

¾ pound *cooked* bacon

1¾ cups mayonnaise

¾ cup sugar

½ cup cider vinegar

1. Chop the broccoli, cauliflower, eggs, onion and bacon in very small pieces. Add any additional odds and ends you may find in your vegetable drawer in the refrigerator (peppers, radishes, cucumber, etc); place in large container with tight fitting lid.
2. In a medium bowl, combine mayonnaise, sugar and vinegar; whisk.
3. Pour mayonnaise sauce over the chopped veggies. Cover tightly and marinate overnight in the refrigerator.
4. Toss lightly before serving.

HINT: Buy pre-cut veggies at the store for convenience. You could also use bacon bits in place of cooked bacon. Keeps well in refrigerator up to 4 days.

QUICK QUESADILLAS

The ingredients in this recipe should always be in your refrigerator, they could be used in this and many other quick recipes.

Prep time: 2 min.   Broil time: 3 min.   Quantity: 4-6 servings

8 small flour tortillas

⅓ cup cheddar or Monterey Jack cheese, grated

1 tomato, chopped

¼ cup green onions, chopped

Lettuce, chopped

1. Place tortillas on cookie sheet. Spray tops of tortillas lightly with non-stick cooking spray.
2. Place 2 tablespoons cheese on each tortilla and melt under broiler.
3. Remove quickly and top with tomato, lettuce and onion.
4. Fold up and eat.

HINT: Other topping options include: chopped cooked chicken, beef, pork, diced red or green pepper, guacamole, or refried beans.

SWEET AND SPICY GLAZED CHICKEN

Great dinner idea with simple ingredients.

| Prep time: 2 min. | Grill time: 15 min. | Quantity: 4 servings |

4 boneless, skinless chicken breast halves

⅓ cup Dijon mustard

¼ cup apricot preserves

2 teaspoons ground ginger

1 teaspoon dry mustard (optional)

1. In a small bowl, combine mustard, preserves, ground ginger and dry mustard to make glaze; mix well. Spread some glaze on chicken and place on grill.
2. While grilling, frequently baste chicken with remaining glaze.
3. Serve immediately.

HINT: Serve with fresh fruit salad and garlic bread. Make a double batch and freeze half the cooked chicken in a small zip-top storage bag. Use the chicken in any recipe calling for cooked chicken.

CHICKEN TACOS

The combination of onion, garlic and taco seasoning makes for a zesty chicken dish the whole family will enjoy.

Prep time: 2 min.   Cook time: 15 min.   Quantity: 4-6 servings

2 tablespoons vegetable oil

1 medium onion, finely chopped

1 garlic clove, crushed*

2-3 cups cooked chicken, chopped

1 can (15-ounce) tomato puree

1 can (4.5-ounce) chopped green chilies

1 package (1.25-ounce) taco seasoning mix
(40% less sodium works well)

Salt and pepper to taste

Fixings for tortillas

6 tortilla shells, corn or flour

Grated cheeses

Guacamole

Shredded lettuce

Salsa, etc...

1. In large skillet, warm vegetable oil over medium heat; add onion and garlic. Sauté until onion is translucent, about 5 minutes.
2. Add chicken, tomatoes, chilies and taco seasoning to skillet; salt and pepper to taste. Simmer over medium-low heat for 10 minutes; stir occasionally.
3. Serve with tortilla shells and all the fixings.

My friend, Chris Coady, is an incredible cook who is always on the run with her family. She graciously accepted the challenge of testing some recipes. I thank her for her wonderful comments and 'tender' suggestions to help make this recipe and this cookbook 'taste great'!

*Use chopped or minced ready to use garlic in the jar for convenience.

15-MINUTE CHICKEN AND RICE

Many of you may have a recipe similar to this one, but for those of you who don't—this is a keeper! Simple, easy and mild.

Prep time: 5 min.   Cook time: 15 min.   Quantity: 4 servings

2 tablespoons vegetable oil

4 boneless, skinless chicken breast halves, cut into 1-inch chunks

1 can (10¾-ounce) cream of chicken soup

2 cups broccoli, chopped

1 cup water

¼ teaspoon pepper

¼ teaspoon paprika (optional)

1½ cups **_uncooked_** instant rice

1. In a large skillet, warm oil over medium-high heat. Add chicken to skillet and season with salt and pepper. Cook until brown on both sides, 8-10 minutes or until juices run clear.
2. While chicken is cooking—chop the broccoli!
3. Remove chicken from pan and place on platter; cover to keep warm.
4. Add soup, water, pepper and paprika to same large skillet; bring to a boil. Stir in rice, broccoli and chicken; reduce heat to medium-low.
5. Cover tightly and cook over low heat for 5 minutes or until chicken is warmed through.

HINT: You can add 1-2 tablespoons of water if you prefer a slightly moister dish. This dish can be rewarmed, or frozen and reheated for a quick meal any time!

FAST FAJITAS

Easy—quick—good!

Prep time: 5 min.   Cook time: 8-10 min.   Quantity: 4-6 servings

3 boneless, skinless chicken breast halves; cut into thin ½-inch strips

½ large green pepper, sliced thin

1 small onion, sliced thin

1 can (4.5-ounce) chopped green chilies

½ teaspoon crushed garlic* (use ½ teaspoon garlic powder in a pinch)

1 package (1.25-ounce) fajita seasoning mix

8-10 flour tortillas

Lettuce, shredded

1 cup cheddar cheese, grated (optional)

1. In a large fry pan, sauté chicken, green pepper, onion, chilies, garlic and fajita seasoning on medium-high heat for 8-10 minutes; stirring frequently.
2. Fill flour tortillas with chicken mixture, top with cheese and lettuce.
3. Serve.

Use chopped or minced ready to use garlic in the jar for convenience.

CHAMP HOAGIE

Nothing beats the taste of a homemade hoagie sandwich. It takes only 5 minutes to put it together, and the taste is 100 times better than the store-bought version. The hoagie can be made in the morning if needed, and refrigerated until evening activities.

Prep time: 5 min.	Cook time: none	Quantity: 6 servings

1 large loaf Italian bread

4 ounces Swiss cheese, sliced

4 ounces salami, thinly sliced

4 ounces ham, thinly sliced

4 ounces mozzarella or provolone, sliced

1 small tomato, thinly sliced

Shredded lettuce

Italian salad dressing (zesty kind)

Follow the instructions specifically to achieve the great flavor, especially if the hoagie will be sitting in the fridge during the day!

1. Slice bread in half, lengthwise; layer the Swiss cheese, salami, ham and mozzarella on bottom half of bread.
2. Place tomato on top of cheese; sprinkle dressing over the tomatoes.
3. Place lettuce on top of dressing; cover with top of bread.
4. You can slice into 6 servings and wrap individually or wrap whole and cut later.

FRESH FLAVOR TURKEY BURGERS

Awesome flavor. My husband (who is not a ground turkey lover) thought these burgers were the best he has ever had! Pan-fry these tender patties—do not grill!

Prep time: 8 min.	Cook time: 8 min.	Quantity: 4 burgers

1 pound lean ground turkey

¼ cup fresh mint, chopped**

1 bunch green onions, minced

¼ cup Parmesan cheese

2 large garlic cloves, crushed*

2 tablespoons olive oil

Salt and pepper to taste

1. Combine all the above ingredients except the olive oil; form into 4 patties.
2. In a large skillet, warm oil over medium-high heat. Pan fry about 5 minutes on each side or until meat is cooked through.
3. Salt and pepper to taste; serve on hamburger buns.

HINT: Patties can be made ahead and refrigerated until ready to fry.

*Use chopped or minced ready to use garlic in the jar for convenience.
**Mint can be found in the produce section at your local grocery store.

TASTY SEASONED BURGERS

This is one quick & easy way to make the perfect burger even better.

| Prep time: 5 min. | Cook time: 10 min. | Quantity: 4-6 burgers |

1½ pounds ground beef

½ teaspoon salt

¼ teaspoon black pepper

2 tablespoons Italian bread crumbs

¾ teaspoon garlic powder

2 teaspoons Worcestershire sauce

2 teaspoons A-1® steak sauce

1. In a large bowl, combine all above ingredients; form into 4-6 patties.
2. Grill, broil, or pan fry. You don't even need ketchup!

HINT: Remember—the less you handle the meat while mixing ingredients and making patties, the more tender your burgers will be!

FIELD BURGERS

Juicy, tasty and perfect with ketchup and a hard roll in the back yard after work.

| Prep time: 2 min. | Cook time: 8 min. | Quantity: 4 burgers |

1 package (1-ounce) ranch salad dressing mix

1 pound ground beef

1. Mix both ingredients together; form into 4 patties.
2. Grill, broil or fry and serve on hard rolls.

HINT: Remember—the less you handle the meat while mixing ingredients and making patties, the more tender your burgers will be!

HAMBURGER CRUMBLE

Another great idea for ground beef. The meat is so tender and flaky that it crumbles in the pan. Serve with rice or buttered noodles and the kids will undoubtedly ask for seconds. I suggest that you make a double batch—one to eat and one to freeze!

Prep time: 5 min.   Cook time: 10 min.   Quantity: 6-8 servings

1½ pounds ground meat

½ cup mayonnaise

4-6 tablespoons chopped onion

2 teaspoons chili powder

½ teaspoon salt

1. In a large bowl, mix all ingredients listed above. Place in frying pan and sauté over medium-high heat until meat is no longer pink and onions are tender, about 10–12 minutes.
2. Serve.

HINT: Make crumble and place in refrigerator up to 1 day in advance or freeze for another time.

SLEEPING DOGS

This recipe is a classic, but I decided to include it because it is a hit with kids. My kids named it 'sleeping dogs' because of the blanket of dough around the hotdog. These are great for a birthday party or a sleepover when the kids never stop eating and you want to surprise them with something fun.

Prep time: 5 min.	Bake time: 375°/13 min.	Quantity: 4-8 servings

8 hotdogs

4-8 slices American cheese, each sliced into thirds

1 container (8-ounce) crescent dough

1. Preheat oven to 375 degrees.
2. Slit hotdogs lengthwise making a pocket (not cutting all the way through).
3. Stuff each hotdog with 2-3 pieces of cheese. Wrap each hotdog with crescent triangle. Place on cookie sheet—cheese side up.
4. Bake for 13-15 minutes or until golden brown.

GREEK PORK PITA POCKETS

This is so quick and easy. Set the marinade up before you leave for work or as soon as you get home. Either way, this tasty meal will be ready to cook in a flash.

| Prep time: 10 min. | Marinate time: 1-8 hrs. | Cook time: 3-5 min. | Quantity: 4 servings |

1 pound pork loin chops, cut into ¼-inch thick strips

4 tablespoons olive oil

4 tablespoons lemon juice

1 tablespoon prepared mustard

2 large garlic cloves, crushed*

1 teaspoon oregano

2 pita rounds, cut in half

Toppings

Chopped red onion

Shredded lettuce

Cucumber sauce (recipe follows)

1. In a non-porous bowl, combine the olive oil, lemon juice, mustard, garlic and oregano; whisk well. Add the meat to above mixture and toss to coat. Refrigerate for 1-8 hours.
2. In a large skillet, warm ***1 tablespoon vegetable oil*** over high heat. Pour the meat and its marinade into skillet and stir-fry 4-6 minutes.
3. Serve meat in warm pita pockets with lettuce, red onion and cucumber sauce (recipe follows).

*Use chopped or minced ready to use garlic in the jar for convenience.

131

CUCUMBER SAUCE

This is a perfect accompaniment to the previous recipe. Delicious with any grilled pork or chicken dish.

Prep time: 3 min.	Cook time: none	Quantity: approx. 2 cups

1 cup plain yogurt

1 cucumber, peeled and chopped in small pieces

½ teaspoon garlic powder

½ teaspoon dill

1. Mix together and refrigerate until ready to serve.

MODERN MAMMA'S PIEROGI

*You can find the pierogi in the frozen food section of most any grocery store. They are **so** easy to make. I always keep a stash of them in the freezer.*

Prep time: 2 min.   Cook time: 5 min.   Quantity: 4 servings

1 box frozen pierogi, your favorite filling

1-2 large onions

4 tablespoons butter

1. In a large skillet, sauté onions in butter, about 3-4 minutes.
2. Place frozen pierogi in a large pot of boiling water; boil for 3-5 minutes; drain.
3. In a large bowl, toss onions and butter with pierogi.
4. Serve.

HINT: You can top pierogi with stir-fried vegetables or place the boiled pierogi in the stir-fry with the vegetables for crispier pierogi.

BBQ SALMON FILLETS

A pleasant barbeque flavor that doesn't overpower the flavor of the fish.

Prep time: 2 min.   Cook time: 10 min.   Quantity: 4 servings

1 pound salmon fillet

2 tablespoons mayonnaise

¼ cup barbecue sauce

1 teaspoon Worcestershire sauce

⅛ teaspoon hot sauce

1 teaspoon lemon juice

1 tablespoon brown sugar or honey

1. In a small bowl, combine all ingredients except salmon.
2. Bring salmon to room temperature. Baste fish with sauce and broil or grill for about 10 minutes or until salmon is tender and cooked through.
3. Serve immediately.

HINT: Remember to baste fish occasionally during broiling or grilling.

THE BEST OATMEAL EVER

If anyone in the family likes dried fruit, then fill them up with this one. It is incredibly tasty, easy to make and loaded with valuable nutrients.

| Prep time: 2 min. | Microwave time: 5 min. | Quantity: 2 servings |

½ cup whole oats

1 cup milk

pinch of salt

Place oats and milk in a microwaveable bowl and microwave on high for three minutes. Then use one of the following options:

- 1 small ripe banana, 1 tablespoon maple syrup and 2-4 tablespoons chopped nuts.
- Stir into cooked oatmeal.

OR

- ¼ cup dried cut-up figs, prunes or raisins; stir into oatmeal one minute into cook time.
- Top with 2 tablespoons apricot jam before serving.

OR

- 1 small ripe pear cored and cut up and 2 tablespoons crystallized ginger cut into small pieces.
- Stir into cooked oatmeal.

HINT: Remember to use a bowl at least twice the volume of the ingredients so you don't have a boil over in your microwave—keep an eye on the stuff. For those of you (and you know who you are) who have been making oatmeal on the stove—keep on making it on the stove!

30 MINUTE DISHES

Close to 30 minutes of prep and cook time before you serve
the meal. That is the idea behind every recipe in this chapter.
These dishes will need a side dish, salad or bread, which
can be prepared at the same time. Everyone will be happy,
full, and glad you didn't miss the violin lesson!

30-Minute Dishes

PEANUT BUTTER CHICKEN

A mild peanut butter flavor gives this chicken versatility with any kind of side dish!

| Prep time: 3 min. | Cook time: 30 min. | Quantity: 4-6 servings |

½ cup peanut oil

3½ pounds boneless skinless chicken (preferably thighs) cut into 2-3-inch chunks

2 large onions, chopped

½ cup peanut butter, creamy or crunchy

2 cups water

¼ teaspoon cayenne pepper

Salt to taste

Chopped peanuts (optional)

1. In a large skillet, warm oil over medium-high heat. Add chicken to skillet and cook until brown and tender on all sides; turn occasionally, about 10 minutes. Transfer chicken to platter and keep warm.
2. Pour off all but 2 tablespoons of oil from skillet. Reduce heat to medium; add onions and cook for 5 minutes or until soft.
3. Stir in peanut butter, water and cayenne pepper; salt to taste; whisk until combined. Return chicken to skillet and simmer until sauce slightly thickens, about 8-10 minutes.
4. Garnish with chopped peanuts and serve.

HINT: Serve alone or over pasta or rice.

CINNAMON CHICKEN

A sweet and savory seasoned dish that goes well with steamed rice and broccoli. Kids love the taste.

Prep time: 10 min.   Cook time: 25 min.   Quantity: 4 servings

4 boneless skinless chicken breast halves

¼ teaspoon cinnamon

¼ teaspoon cloves

¼ teaspoon salt

¼ teaspoon pepper

3 tablespoons vegetable oil

1 large onion chopped

2 garlic cloves, crushed*

¾ cup orange juice

2 tablespoons raisins

1. Pat chicken dry with paper towels. Combine cinnamon, cloves, salt and pepper in small bowl.
2. Season chicken on both sides with seasoning mix.
3. In a large skillet, warm oil over medium heat. Add chicken to skillet and cook until brown, about 8 minutes.
4. Turn chicken over; add onion and garlic to skillet. Brown second side of chicken while stirring onions and garlic frequently, another 8 minutes.
5. Add orange juice and raisins to skillet; reduce heat to low. Cover and cook for 10 minutes or until juices run clear when chicken is pierced.
6. Serve.

Use chopped or minced ready to use garlic in the jar for convenience.

PAN FRIED ITALIAN CHICKEN

When it is cold outside and I don't feel like grilling, I cook this dish. It has a simple Mediterranean flavor. Serve with steamed green beans tossed with almonds and Italian salad dressing and a fresh loaf of bread.

Prep time: 5 min.	Cook time: 20 min.	Quantity: 4 servings

6 tablespoons butter, room temperature

1 green onion, finely chopped

1-2 teaspoons garlic, crushed*

1 teaspoon lemon juice

1 teaspoon sage

¼ teaspoon pepper

¼ teaspoon salt

4 boneless, skinless chicken breast halves

1. In food processor, combine butter, green onion, garlic, lemon juice, sage, pepper and salt; process until smooth, about 10 seconds.
2. Heat large skillet over medium-high heat. Pat the chicken breasts dry with paper towel; spread half of the herb-butter spread on one side of chicken breasts.
3. Place chicken in skillet (herb-butter side down) and fry for 8-10 minutes. Spread other half of herb-butter on chicken, while in skillet. Turn chicken over and fry for 8-10 minutes or when juices run clear when chicken is pierced.
4. Serve immediately.

*Use chopped or minced ready to use garlic in the jar for convenience.

EASTERN BEEF

Great recipe—even better marinade! This marinade works well with chicken, too.

Prep time: 5 min.   Marinate time: 6-12 hrs.   Grill time: desired doneness   Quantity: 4 servings

2-3 bunches green onions, chopped

½ cup soy sauce

½ cup water

½ cup sugar

⅓ cup sesame seeds

4 medium cloves garlic, crushed*

½ teaspoon black pepper

1½-2 pounds bottom round of beef, sliced ¼-½-inch thick

1. In a freezer type zip-top bag or plastic storage container with tight fitting lid, combine all the above ingredients except the beef; mix well.
2. Add meat to the marinade and refrigerate 6-12 hours.
3. Grill until desired doneness.

HINT: Garnish with chopped green onion and serve with rice and steamed veggies. My mom used a whole roast for this recipe and grilled it on a spit, then sliced the meat before serving—it turned out great!

*Use chopped or minced ready to use garlic in the jar for convenience.

TEXAS RANCH STEAK

This has a great seasoned flavor when grilled. Serve with Texas garlic bread and a crisp green salad.

| Prep time: 5 min. | Grill time: 16 min. | Quantity: 4 servings |

1 package (1-ounce) ranch salad dressing mix

1½ tablespoons water

2 tablespoons olive oil

1½ pounds flank steak

1. In a small bowl, combine dressing mix, water and olive oil with a wooden spoon to make a paste.
2. Coat one side of steak with half the paste. Place coated side over hot coals and grill for 7-8 minutes. Coat top side of meat with remaining paste while grilling. Turn meat over and grill an additional 7-8 minutes.
3. Remove from grill and serve immediately.

HINT: If you want your meat cooked more than medium rare, increase the grilling times by 1 minute on each side.

QUICKEST MEATLOAF IN THE WEST

A meatloaf dinner is a classic and this recipe makes it faster then quick. The microwave is the key here and it tastes and looks like it came from the oven! This was my mother-in-law's favorite standby and I have modified it over the years for our faster lifestyle.

| Prep time: 10 min. | Microwave time: approx. 20 min. | Quantity: 4 servings |

Meatloaf Ingredients

1 pound lean ground meat

1 large egg

¼ cup milk

½ cup oatmeal

1 small onion, chopped

¼ cup ketchup

2 teaspoons prepared mustard

½ teaspoon salt

½ teaspoon pepper

Glaze

2 tablespoons brown sugar

2 tablespoons ketchup

Mustard

1. In a large bowl, combine all the 'meatloaf ingredients'.
2. Coat a microwaveable baking dish with non-stick cooking spray.
3. Pat meat mixture into baking dish making loaf approximately 2-3-inch high.
4. Cook uncovered on high for 14 minutes; drain any liquid that gathers in bottom of baking dish and discard.
5. In small bowl combine the 'glaze'; spread over meat.
6. Cook on high for 5 more minutes.
7. Let stand for 5 minutes before slicing and serving.

HINT: This can be cooked and frozen, then re-warmed when needed. Great cold and sliced for sandwiches the next day, so think about making two!

"I rarely use my microwave to cook meat, but this was very good and quick! I doubled the glaze which the kids loved. A+" —Eddie Jones.

GRILLED PORK

Another great fool-proof marinade I use all the time for pork.

Prep time: 2 min.   Marinate time: 4-8 hrs.   Grill time: 15-20 min.   Quantity: 4 servings

½ cup soy sauce

½ cup orange juice

1 teaspoon ground ginger (¼ teaspoon minced fresh ginger)

2 large garlic cloves, crushed*

2 (¾ pound each) pork tenderloins

1. In a non-porous container or large freezer type zip-top bag, combine soy sauce, orange juice, ginger and garlic.
2. Add meat to marinade and refrigerate 4-8 hours, turning occasionally if you can.
3. Remove meat from marinade and place on hot grill; discard marinade.
4. Grill meat until inside temperature is 160 degrees, turning meat frequently while grilling.
5. Remove meat from grill; slice and serve immediately.

HINT: Serve with a fresh green salad and rolls.

*Use chopped or minced ready to use garlic in the jar for convenience.

ASIAN PORK CHOPS

Another one of those microwave dishes that no one will believe came out of the microwave. It has a wonderful Asian flavor and can be served over rice, couscous, or pasta.

> Prep time: 5 min.   Microwave time: 15 min.   Quantity: 4 servings

1 tablespoon ground ginger

2 large cloves garlic, crushed*

¼ cup ketchup

3 tablespoons soy sauce

2 teaspoons cornstarch

Dash of red pepper flakes

4 (½–¾-inch thick each) pork chops or cutlets

1 can (20-ounce) pineapple chunks, drained (reserve liquid)

3 tablespoons chopped green onions

2 tablespoons toasted sesame seeds

Salt and pepper to taste

1. In a microwaveable casserole dish, combine pineapple juice, ginger, garlic, ketchup, soy sauce, cornstarch and red pepper flakes; whisk until lumps are gone.
2. Place pork chops in casserole dish; cover with plastic wrap.
3. Microwave on high for 6 minutes; stir slightly and add pineapple chunks.
4. Microwave for 5 more minutes (rotating dish if not on a microwave turntable).
5. Remove and let sit, covered, for 2-3 minutes.
6. Sprinkle with onions and sesame seeds; salt and pepper to taste and serve.

HINT: This dish is great with a side of instant rice and French cut green beans!

*Use chopped or minced ready to use garlic in the jar for convenience.

30-Minute Dishes

SAN ANTONIO PORK CUTLETS

A great dish packed with flavor and texture. Perfect when you run out of good ideas for dinner. Don't let the list of ingredients scare you away. The procedure is very easy and the total time is less than half an hour from start to table.

| Prep time: 10 min. | Cook time: 15 min. | Quantity: 4 servings |

4 (½–¾-inch thick each) pork chops or loins

1 teaspoon garlic salt

1 teaspoon ground cumin

2 tablespoons vegetable oil

1 red bell pepper, cored, seeded, chopped ½-inch pieces

3 green onions, chopped

1 clove garlic, crushed*

1 cup frozen whole kernel corn, thawed

1 avocado, chopped

1 tablespoon cilantro (optional)

1 teaspoon lime juice

1. Rub both sides of pork chops with garlic salt and cumin.
2. In a large skillet, warm oil over medium heat. Add meat to skillet and sauté for 5 minutes per side, or until fully cooked. Remove meat from skillet; place on serving platter and keep warm.
3. Increase heat to medium-high. Add pepper, onion, garlic and corn to same skillet and cook 3-5 minutes.
4. Remove skillet from heat and stir in avocado, cilantro and lime juice; pour over meat and serve.

*Use chopped or minced ready to use garlic in the jar for convenience.

FLEXIBLE MARINADE

This is great for the grill when you are tired of chicken and burgers.

| Prep time: 2 min. | Marinate time: 2-24 hrs. | Grill time: 20 min. | Quantity: 4-6 servings |

1-1½ pounds lean pork, cut into 2-inch cubes

2 large garlic cloves, crushed*

¼ cup soy sauce

1 tablespoon honey

1 teaspoon chili powder

1. In freezer type zip-top bag or a non-porous container, combine the above ingredients and marinate 2-24 hours.
2. Remove pork from marinade (reserving marinade) and thread pork cubes on skewers; grill over hot coals for 20 minutes, turning occasionally.
3. You can brush the meat the first 10 minutes of cooking with the reserved marinade juices if desired. (Discard remaining marinade.)

HINT: Serve with fresh veggies with dip and French bread.

*Use chopped or minced ready to use garlic in the jar for convenience.

SPEEDY GONZALES CHILI

This is the quickest method of making chili besides opening up a can. My friend, Lauren, tested this recipe and used a veggie protein mix instead of using animal products and put it all in a crock-pot (which I never thought of) and found it to be exceptional!

| Prep time: 10 min. | Cook time: 20 min. | Quantity: 4 servings |

1 pound ground meat, beef, turkey, or chicken

1 medium onion, chopped

1-2 cans (15-ounce each) red kidney beans, drained

½ teaspoon garlic powder

1 can (10½-ounce) condensed tomato soup

⅔ cup water

¾ teaspoon salt

1 tablespoon chili powder

1. In a large skillet over medium-high heat, fry meat and onion until meat is lightly browned; remove any grease, if necessary.
2. Add remaining ingredients to skillet as listed; stir well.
3. Bring to a boil; lower heat, cover and simmer for 20 minutes, stirring occasionally.

HINT: Serve with crackers, grated cheese, shredded lettuce, chopped green onions or rice.

CHILI CHEESE CASSEROLE

Great dish that is not a 'soupy' chili.

| Prep time: 8 min. | Bake time: 375°/20-25 min. | Quantity: 4 servings |

1 can (15-ounce) chili

1 medium onion, chopped

3 handfuls of Fritos® corn chips (divided)

1 cup cheddar cheese, grated

1. Preheat oven to 375 degrees.
2. Coat 8x8-inch baking pan with non-stick cooking spray.
3. Spread 2 handfuls of chips on bottom of baking pan.
4. In a small bowl, combine the chili and onion; spread on top of chips.
5. Top chili mixture with 1 more additional handful of chips.
6. Bake for 20 to 25 minutes. Sprinkle cheese on top of chips and bake 3-5 more minutes.
7. Serve.

SASSY HAWAIIAN PORK BURGERS

The kids really like the pineapple slices, which add just the right amount of sweetness!

Prep time: 8 min.   Cook time: 20 min.   Quantity: 8 burgers

1¼-1½ pounds ground pork

1 can (8-ounce) water chestnuts, drained and chopped finely

1 large egg, beaten

2 green onions, chopped

½ teaspoon ginger

¼ teaspoon pepper

6 tablespoons seasoned breadcrumbs

4 tablespoons teriyaki sauce (divided)

½ teaspoon salt

½ teaspoon pepper

1 can (8-ounce) pineapple rings, drained

1. In a large bowl, combine everything except 2 tablespoons of teriyaki sauce and pineapple rings; mix well.
2. Wet hands and form meat mixture into 8 patties.
3. Place patties in **cold** skillet. Fry patties over medium-high heat, about 10 minutes per side; baste occasionally with remaining 2 tablespoons of teriyaki sauce.
4. Serve burgers on large Kaiser rolls with leaf lettuce and pineapple rings.

TURKEY VEGGIE BBQ BURGERS

You control the spice in this burger with the type of BBQ sauce you use.

Prep time: 10 min.   Cook time: 14 min.   Quantity: 4-5 burgers

1¼ pounds ground turkey

½ cup zucchini, grated and patted dry with paper towels

1 bunch green onions, chopped

3 tablespoons barbecue sauce

2 tablespoons bread crumbs

1 teaspoon chili powder

1 large garlic clove, crushed*

1 teaspoon each salt and pepper

3 tablespoons vegetable oil

Extra barbecue sauce for basting

1. In a large bowl, combine all ingredients (except vegetable oil and extra barbecue sauce); mix well and form into 4-5 patties.
2. In a large skillet, warm vegetable oil over medium-high heat.
3. Cook patties in skillet approximately 7-8 minutes per side, basting patties with barbecue sauce occasionally.

HINT #1: Great served with coleslaw and baked beans. My son actually puts the slaw on the burger. Try this—it's awesome!

HINT #2: To cook on grill—freeze burgers and place on grill frozen (to keep from falling apart).

*Use chopped or minced ready to use garlic in the jar for convenience.

RED BEAN BURGERS

These burgers are hands down better than the store bought variety and easy, too.

Prep time: 8 min.　　Cook time 15 min.　　Quantity: 6 burgers

2 cans (15-ounce each) red kidney beans, rinsed and drained

½ cup bread crumbs, plain or seasoned

4 green onions, minced

2 large eggs

1 tablespoon soy sauce

1 teaspoon ground ginger

1 teaspoon garlic, crushed*

2 tablespoons vegetable oil

1. In a large bowl mash beans; add breadcrumbs, green onions, eggs, soy sauce, ginger and garlic. Mix thoroughly and form into 6 patties.
2. In a large skillet, warm oil over medium heat. Cook patties, about 6-8 minutes on each side or until dark brown and crispy.
3. Serve on buns with lettuce, cucumber, tomato and 'special sauce' (see recipe below).

Special Sauce

¼ cup mayonnaise

1 tablespoon horseradish

1 tablespoon green onion, minced

1 teaspoon soy sauce

Mix together and refrigerate until ready to serve.

Use chopped or minced ready to use garlic in the jar for convenience.

RED BEANS AND RICE

Great for the vegetarian in the family. You can add spicy sausage at step #2 for the meat lover.

Prep time: 5 min.	Cook time: 30 min.	Quantity: 6 servings

2 tablespoons olive oil

1 large onion, thinly sliced

2 cloves garlic, crushed*

1 green pepper, chopped (red or yellow can be used)

1 can (32-ounce) peeled whole tomatoes, chopped

1 medium tomato, chopped

½ teaspoon each basil, oregano, thyme and chili powder

2 cans (15-ounce each) kidney beans, drained

Salt and pepper to taste

1. In a large skillet, warm oil over medium heat; add onion and garlic and sauté for 5 minutes.
2. Add pepper to skillet and sauté for 5 minutes.
3. Add canned and fresh tomato and seasonings to skillet; simmer for 15 minutes.
4. Add beans to skillet; simmer 5 more minutes.
5. Serve over rice.

HINT: Brown rice adds a great flavor to this dish if you have a little extra time to prepare it. My friend, Lauren Marinez, 'from way back when we moved to Lansing' tested this recipe. She is a great cook and can put anything together in a snap. She is also a wealth of knowledge when it comes to 'beans and rice dishes' as well as feeding picky kids and picky adults! She suggested using pinto beans in place of kidney beans. She finds that kids and adults like them better than kidney beans. Thanks, Lauren, for the great hint!

*Use chopped or minced ready to use garlic in the jar for convenience.

TOMATO CHEESE PIE

A very cheesy rich dish that is great for pot-lucks.

| Prep time: 8 min. | Bake time: 325°/20 min. | Quantity: 4-6 servings |

1 – 9-inch pre-baked pie shell

1 cup cheddar cheese, grated

1 cup mozzarella cheese, grated

1 cup ricotta cheese (**_not_** low-fat)

¼ pound mushrooms, sliced

½ small onion, chopped

1 large tomato, thinly sliced

2 teaspoons Italian seasoning

1 bunch green onions, chopped

Salt and pepper to taste

1. Preheat oven to 325 degrees.
2. In a large bowl, combine cheddar, mozzarella cheese, ricotta cheese, mushrooms and onions; mix well.
3. Spoon cheese mixture into pie shell; top with tomato and sprinkle with Italian seasoning, green onions, salt and pepper.
4. Bake 20 minutes. Cool for 5 minutes before slicing.

HINT: A six-ounce can of salmon or tuna can be mixed in with the cheeses for a new twist. Remember to use pre-grated cheese and ready-sliced mushrooms to speed up the prep time.

CHEESE PIE

My daughter loves this pie because it tastes like pizza without the sauce.

Prep time: 5 min.	Bake time: 425°/20 min.	Quantity: 4-6 servings	Broil time: 2 min.

1½ cups milk

3 large eggs

1¼ cups Bisquick®

⅓ cup Parmesan cheese, grated

½ teaspoon salt

¼ teaspoon pepper

¾ cup mozzarella cheese, cubed

1 medium tomato, sliced

½ cup mozzarella cheese, grated

1. Preheat oven to 425 degrees.
2. Coat a 10-inch pie pan with non-stick cooking spray.
3. In a large bowl, combine milk, eggs, Bisquick®, Parmesan cheese, salt and pepper; whisk for 1 minute. Pour mixture into pie pan and sprinkle with mozzarella cubes.
4. Bake pie for 20 minutes or until puffy and golden brown.
5. Remove pie from oven and preheat broiler. Place tomato slices on top of pie (it will seem high but the tomatoes don't fall off), and top with mozzarella cheese. Broil for 2 minutes or until cheese melts and is bubbly.
6. Cool 5 minutes before slicing.

INCREDIBLE TOMATO TART

This recipe is very easy and the rich taste will seem like you labored for hours.

| Prep time: 8 min. | Bake time: 375°/35 min. | Quantity: 8 servings |

1 – 9-inch baked pie shell

2 medium tomatoes, sliced

8 ounces ricotta cheese (*not* low-fat)

cup Monterey Jack cheese, grated

cup mozzarella cheese, grated

2 large eggs, slightly beaten

1 teaspoon basil

1 teaspoon oregano

teaspoon garlic powder

teaspoon onion powder

teaspoon black pepper

2 tablespoons Parmesan cheese, grated

1. Preheat oven to 375 degrees.
2. In the pie shell, layer half of the tomatoes.
3. In a large bowl, combine ricotta, Monterey Jack and mozzarella cheeses, eggs, basil, oregano, garlic powder, onion powder and black pepper; stir with fork until well combined.
4. Spoon cheese mixture on top of layered tomatoes; top with remaining tomato slices and sprinkle with Parmesan cheese.
5. Bake pie until filling is set and golden brown, about 30 minutes.
6. Cool 5 minutes before slicing.

ROLLATTA FRITTATA

I remember my Mom making frittatas when she was short on dinner ideas, had to use up left-over vegetables from the evening before, or when she was in a pinch for time. This is an easy dish based on my Mom's original recipe that can be made with very little preparation and no need to run to the store for special ingredients.

Prep time: 5 min.	Cook time: 20 min.	Quantity: 6 servings

6–8 tablespoons margarine

3 medium russet potatoes, peeled and sliced to ¼-inch thickness

3 tablespoons all-purpose flour

½ teaspoon garlic powder

½ teaspoon Italian seasoning

8 large eggs

¼ cup grated Parmesan cheese

Salt and pepper to taste

1. In a large skillet, melt margarine over medium high heat.
2. In a large bowl, toss potato slices with flour, garlic powder and Italian seasonings. Place in skillet and cook covered until potatoes are tender; stir often, about 10-12 minutes.
3. In the same large bowl, beat eggs slightly with Parmesan cheese, salt and pepper. Reduce heat to medium and pour the egg mixture over potatoes. Re-adjust potatoes or tip pan to allow uncooked egg to flow under the potato; about 1 minute.
4. Do not stir the eggs. Cover skillet with lid and cook until eggs are set. This will take 8-10 minutes.
5. Loosen frittata from pan with spatula and gently slide onto serving platter.
6. Serve with toast and fresh fruit salad.

HINT: I have placed all kinds of things in the skillet with the potatoes including onion, green peppers and even cooked rice or pasta. This is a basic recipe that can be modified to suit your family's tastes.

FAST BRUNCH EGGS

Fast and easy dish. Serve with fresh orange or apple slices and toast.

Prep time: 5 min.   Bake time: 350°/25 min.   Quantity: 4 servings

5 large eggs, beaten

2 cups cheddar cheese

1 cup cottage cheese

½ stick margarine

¼ cup all-purpose flour

½ teaspoon baking powder

⅛ teaspoon salt

1. Preheat oven to 350 degrees.
2. Coat an 8x8-inch ovenproof **glass** baking dish* with non-stick cooking spray.
3. In a large bowl, combine all the ingredients; mix well.
4. Pour into baking dish and bake 25-30 minutes or until golden brown and butter knife inserted in center comes out clean.
5. Let rest for 5 minutes before serving.

HINT: You can add to the egg mixture olives, artichokes, green chilies or even thin slices of pepperoni for a different flavor. This may alter the cooking time slightly.

If baking in standard metal or ceramic baking pan, increase oven temperature by 25 degrees.

SUNSHINE CHICKEN KABOBS

The chicken has such a fresh and light taste when prepared like this. Kids really like eating kabobs. This recipe is so easy I bet you will make it a number of times this summer for your family!

Prep time: 10 min.   Marinate time: 30 min.   Grill time: 20 min.   Quantity: approx. 9 – 8-inch skewers

2 pounds boneless, skinless chicken breasts or thighs, cut into 1½-inch cubes

2 green peppers, cut into 2-inch chunks

2 medium onions, cut into quarters

Marinade

½ cup lemon juice

½ cup lime juice

½ cup orange juice

¼ cup honey

1 teaspoon salt

1. In a medium bowl, combine marinade ingredients; whisk well.
2. Add chicken to marinade; coat well. Refrigerate for 30 minutes.
3. Drain chicken and discard marinade. Skewer chicken, peppers and onions on 8-inch skewers.
4. Grill until meat is fully cooked, approximately 8 minutes.

HINT: You can alternate other types of vegetables such as mushrooms and/or zucchini with the chicken on the skewers or you can cook the vegetables on the side.

SWEET GLAZED CHICKEN

A great glaze to put together an hour or two before the cook time, just enough time to take a bike ride with the kids, walk the dog, or do a load of laundry.

| Prep time: 5 min. | Marinate time: 1-2 hours | Grill time: 15 min. | Quantity: 4 servings |

4 boneless, skinless chicken breast halves

Marinade

½ cup honey mustard

3 tablespoons teriyaki sauce, any type

1. In a medium re-sealable container, combine mustard and teriyaki sauce with a whisk. Reserve ⅓ cup of marinade at this time and set aside.
2. Add chicken to marinade, turning to coat all sides of chicken. Seal and refrigerate for 1-2 hours; turn chicken occasionally if possible.
3. Remove chicken from marinade; discard this marinade.
4. Grill chicken for 8 minutes on each side or until juices run clear. Baste with reserved marinade while grilling.
5. Serve with steamed vegetables and rice.

HINT: You can freeze the chicken in the marinade, thaw in the refrigerator the day of serving and grill that evening.

ONE DISH MAIN DISH

This chapter is dedicated to easy dishes that can be made without worrying about the need for much more than a salad or a loaf of bread to compliment the meal. Many of these meals can be made ahead and refrigerated or frozen and re-heated when ready to serve!

PEPPER SPUD AND SAUSAGE

I have been eating this dish since I was a child! I made the recipe a little bit easier and everyone thinks it tastes just as good. I sometimes put this in the oven on a slightly lower temperature (325 degrees) and take the kids to the game. When we come home the dinner is done!

| Prep time: 15 min. | Bake time: 375°/50 min. | Quantity: 6 servings |

2-3 pounds russet potatoes, peeled, cut in ½-inch slices

2 pounds Italian sausage, uncooked, cut into 1-inch pieces

3 green peppers, seeded and sliced thickly

2 large onions, chopped

2 tablespoons olive oil

Salt and pepper to taste

1. Preheat oven to 375 degrees.
2. Coat a large 9x13-inch glass baking dish with non-stick cooking spray.
3. Combine potatoes, sausage, green peppers, onions, olive oil, salt and pepper in baking dish; toss well.
4. Bake uncovered for 50 minutes or until potatoes are tender. (If you have the time—stir occasionally.)
5. Serve immediately.

HINT: Great with a simple green salad!

One Dish Main Dish

CHOP-CHOP MEAL-IN-ONE

I like to make this meal in the summer when we camp because it gives me more time to spend with the kids at the beach, hiking or fishing.

| Prep time: 10 min. | Grill time: 30 min. | Quantity: 6-8 servings |

6-8 ½–¾-inch thick pork loin cutlets

1 large sweet onion

2 large fresh tomatoes

1 green pepper

Garlic powder, salt, pepper, vegetable oil **OR** zesty Italian salad dressing

1. Cut 6-8 pieces of heavy duty foil about 16-inch long; lay on counter.
2. Rub each side of pork cutlet with garlic powder, salt, pepper and vegetable oil **OR** Italian dressing and place each on its own piece of foil.
3. Slice onion and green pepper into 6-8 slices; place one slice of onion and green pepper on top of each cutlet.
4. Slice tomatoes into 12-16 slices and lay 2 slices on top of each green pepper.
5. Season again with garlic powder, salt and pepper **OR** Italian dressing.
6. Tightly wrap each package and place on grill. Grill for 15 minutes on each side.
7. Serve with a hard roll.

HINT: The packages can be made earlier in the day and refrigerated until ready to grill. Make sure you fold the seams over 2-3 times to keep the juices contained in the packet.

CHICKEN AND BROCCOLI

Great meal to whip up and always good as a leftover the next day.

Prep time: 5 min.   Cook time: 35 min.   Quantity: 4 servings

2 tablespoons margarine

1 package (6.9-ounce) Rice-a-Roni® (chicken flavor)

2 cups water

1 teaspoon dried basil

1 teaspoon dried oregano

4 boneless, skinless chicken breast halves

2-3 cups broccoli florets, or 1 large head of broccoli cut up

1 medium tomato, chopped

1 cup grated cheese, mozzarella or cheddar (optional)

1. In a very large skillet, warm margarine over medium heat. Add Rice-a-Roni® (reserve seasoning packet); sauté until golden brown, about 8 minutes.

2. Add 2 cups of water, seasoning packet, basil, and oregano to the rice; stir gently. Increase heat to high; bring to boil.

3. Place chicken on top of rice, reduce heat to medium-low and cover; simmer for 12 minutes. Turn chicken over (add ¼ cup of water if rice is sticking to pan); stir in broccoli and tomato. Cover and simmer for 10-12 more minutes or until chicken is done.

4. Remove from heat and sprinkle with cheese.

5. Cover for 3 minutes; serve.

CREAM THE TEAM CASSEROLE

If you are a Miracle Whip® fan, this recipe is for you. This is a great dish that can be done ahead of time and then just popped into the oven. It can feed a lot, and can also be doubled for the 'big group'!

Prep time: 15 min.   Refrigeration time: 1-12 hours   Bake time: 375°/1 hour   Quantity: 8 servings

2 cups cubed ham

1 package (10-ounce) frozen chopped broccoli, thawed and drained well

2 cups cheddar cheese, grated

1 package (6-ounce) seasoned croutons

4 large eggs

2 cups milk

1 cup Miracle Whip®

2 tablespoons all-purpose flour

2 teaspoons dry mustard

2 teaspoons dried basil

1. Preheat oven to 375 degrees.
2. Coat a 9x13-inch baking pan with non-stick cooking spray.
3. Layer ham, broccoli, cheese and then croutons in prepared pan.
4. In a medium bowl, combine eggs, milk, Miracle Whip®, flour, mustard and basil; whisk until blended.
5. Pour the egg mixture into baking pan over the croutons.
6. Cover and refrigerate 1-12 hours.
7. Bake uncovered for 1 hour.

GAME WINNING CHOWDER

This great fall chowder is so hearty that it can be a complete meal if it's served with only a salad and crusty bread.

Prep time: 15 min.   Cook time: 15 min.   Quantity: 4 servings

1 pound Italian sausage, spicy or sweet, casings removed

2 tablespoons olive oil

1 large onion, finely chopped

1 red pepper, finely chopped

1 pound potatoes, peeled and cut into ½-inch cubes

1 can (14.5-ounce) chicken broth

2 cups **_whole_** milk

¼ cup all-purpose flour

2 cans (15-ounce) corn kernels including natural juices

1. In a large pot, cook sausage over medium-high heat; break apart sausage while cooking. Cook for 5 minutes or until browned; remove sausage and set aside.
2. Add oil, onion, pepper and potatoes to pot; cover and cook for 5 minutes.
3. In a medium bowl, whisk chicken broth, milk and flour together; add to pot; stir well.
4. Add sausage and 2 cans of corn with their own juices to pot; bring to a boil. Reduce heat to medium-low and simmer for 15 minutes or until potatoes are tender.
5. Serve steaming hot.

HINT: Serve with crusty Italian bread.

One Dish Main Dish

QUICK PASS TUNA DISH

This dish can be done lickety-split. My mother would make this in a pinch, and also sent the recipe with me when I went off to college. I could feed all of my roommates with this one.

| Prep time: 5 min. | Cook time: 10 min. | Quantity: 4 servings |

2 cups water

1 package (3-ounce) Ramen® noodles soup mix, any flavor

1 can (6-ounce) tuna, drained and flaked

1 package (10-ounce) frozen mixed vegetables

3 tablespoons all-purpose flour

1 cup heavy cream or half and half

1. In a large skillet, bring water to a boil. Break up Ramen® noodles and add to water with enclosed seasoning packet, tuna and vegetables; stir; bring to a boil. Reduce heat to medium, cover and simmer for 5 minutes.
2. In a small bowl, whisk flour and cream until combined. Add to skillet; simmer, uncovered, until sauce thickens; stir constantly about 2-3 minutes. Salt and pepper to taste.

HINT: If you are a real tuna lover, try this recipe with two cans of tuna!

CHICKEN CURRY CASSEROLE

Lynn Smolenyak and her family made this dinner for us when we were visiting them in Charlevoix, Michigan. Even though they were building their own home, they made time to visit with friends and serve us a great meal. Lynn prepared this dish earlier in the day and refrigerated it until ready to bake when we arrived.

Prep time: 10 min.   Bake time: 350°/30 min.   Quantity: 6-8 servings

3 packages (10-ounce each) frozen broccoli spears

4 cups _cooked_ chicken, cubed (4-5 chicken breasts halves)

1 can (10.5-ounce) cream of chicken soup

1 cup mayonnaise

1 teaspoon lemon juice

1½ teaspoons curry powder

1½ teaspoons cooking sherry

1½ cups sharp cheddar cheese, grated

1 tablespoon butter, melted

¾ cup herb seasoned stuffing

1. Preheat oven to 350 degrees.
2. Coat 9x13-inch baking dish with non-stick cooking spray.
3. Arrange broccoli in bottom of baking dish; arrange chicken evenly on top.
4. In small bowl combine soup, mayonnaise, lemon juice, curry powder and cooking sherry with whisk.
5. Spoon over meat and spread as evenly as possible—it will be thick; sprinkle with cheese.
6. In a small bowl, mix butter and stuffing; sprinkle over cheese.
7. Bake uncovered for 30 minutes.
8. Serve immediately.

BAKED PASTA

This recipe is great when you have a lot of mouths to feed. If the whole track team is coming over, I suggest that you make two or three!

| Prep time: 20 min. | Bake time: 350°/55 min. | Quantity: 6 servings |

8 ounces elbow macaroni, cooked

1 cup water

1 teaspoon garlic powder (divided)

½ teaspoon onion powder

½ cup mozzarella cheese, grated

1 can (16-ounce) tomato puree

1 tablespoon Italian seasonings

1½ pounds cottage cheese (4% milk-fat), preferably small curd

1. Preheat oven to 350 degrees.
2. Coat a 9x13-inch baking pan with non-stick cooking spray.
3. While boiling elbow macaroni, do the following:

   In a small bowl, combine tomato puree, water, Italian seasoning and ½ teaspoon garlic powder; whisk until combined. In a medium bowl, combine cottage cheese, onion powder and ½ teaspoon garlic powder; mix well.
4. Drain elbow macaroni.
5. Spoon one-third of tomato mixture into baking pan, then layer half of elbow macaroni, all of cottage cheese mixture and another one-third tomato mixture. Add remaining elbow macaroni and cover with remaining tomato mixture.
6. Bake covered for 50 minutes. Remove from oven, uncover casserole and top with cheese.
7. Let stand for 5 minutes. Serve!

HINT: This dish can be assembled and frozen up to 2 months. Increase baking time by 30 minutes or until heated through.

My sister, Cindy, tested this and other recipes—she always gave her dog's opinion too!!! Peaches (the dog) gave this dish 4 paws—that means really good!!!

GREAT CHICKEN CASSEROLE

I created this one night by mistake. Steamed broccoli is a real winning combination with the flavors.

| Prep time: 5 min. | Bake time: 325°/1 hour | Quantity: 4 servings |

1 can (10.5-ounce) cream of mushroom soup

1¾ cups rice, uncooked

1¼ soup cans of water

4 boneless, skinless chicken breast halves

1 tablespoon tarragon

Garlic powder

Salt and pepper

Paprika

1. Preheat oven to 325 degrees.
2. Coat a 9x13-inch baking pan with non-stick cooking spray.
3. In a medium bowl, whisk soup, rice and water together until combined; pour into baking pan.
4. Set chicken on top of rice mixture; sprinkle with tarragon, garlic powder, salt and pepper. Garnish with paprika.
5. Cover tightly with foil and bake for 1 hour.
6. Serve!

TORTILLA CASSEROLE

I am always looking for a good recipe to try without meat. I found this a couple of years ago and made some changes to suit what was in my pantry at the time. It came out great—I hope you try it!

Prep time: 15 min.   Bake time: 350°/30 min.   Quantity: 6 servings

2 tablespoons vegetable oil

2 large onions, chopped

2 large green peppers, chopped

1 can (14½-ounce) diced tomatoes

¾ cup picante sauce

2-3 large garlic cloves, crushed*

2 teaspoons cumin

2 cans (15-ounce each) black beans, drained

12 corn tortillas (6-inch)

2 cups cheddar cheese, grated and divided

Desirable toppings

Diced tomatoes

Chopped green onion

Black olives

Sour cream

Cheddar cheese

1. Preheat oven to 350 degrees.
2. Coat a 9x13-inch baking pan with non-stick cooking spray.
3. In a large skillet, warm oil over medium heat. Combine onions, green peppers, tomatoes, picante sauce, garlic and cumin in skillet and bring to a boil. Reduce heat to medium-low and simmer for 10 minutes; remove from heat and stir in beans.
4. Spread one-third of tomato mixture on bottom of baking pan; top with half of the corn tortillas and add another one-third of the tomato mixture. Cover with remaining tortillas and top with remaining tomato mixture.
5. Cover and bake for 30-35 minutes. Remove from oven, sprinkle with cheese and rest for 5 minutes.
6. Serve with toppings.

*Use chopped or minced ready to use garlic in the jar for convenience.

BLT PIE

I have seen many versions of this recipe over the years. I think that the sharpness of the cheddar cheese combined with the bacon and tomato makes this one the best! The kids will love the novelty of the sandwich in a pie!

> Prep time: 10 min.   Bake time: 350°/35 min.   Quantity: 6 servings

1 – 9-inch regular piecrust shell, unbaked (not deep dish)

8 slices bacon, fried until crisp and crumbled (divided in half)

¾ cup sharp cheddar cheese, grated

1 large tomato, chopped

1 small onion, chopped

1 tablespoon dried parsley

1 large egg

⅔ cup evaporated milk (low-fat optional)

1 small tomato, thinly sliced

Shredded lettuce

1. Bake piecrust following package directions.
2. Preheat oven to 350 degrees.
3. In a small bowl, combine half the bacon, cheese, chopped tomato, onion and parsley; spoon into pie shell.
4. In the same small bowl, beat egg with evaporated milk; pour slowly over bacon/cheese mixture; arrange sliced tomato on top.
5. Bake for 35 minutes; remove from oven and let stand for 10 minutes.
6. Serve with shredded lettuce and remaining bacon.

BEAN CASSEROLE

My sister lived in Arizona for a couple of years and came back with a totally different approach to food and its preparation. This recipe has been modified, based on her recommendation, for ease. It has a southwestern flair that can't be missed.

Prep time: 5 min.	Bake time: 350°/45 min.	Quantity: 6-8 servings

3 boneless, skinless chicken breast halves, cut into 1-inch pieces

1 package (1¼-ounce) taco seasoning

2 large green peppers, chopped

1 large red sweet pepper, chopped

1 package (10-ounce) frozen corn, thawed

1 jar (16-ounce) salsa, spicy

1 can (15-ounce) black beans, drained

1 can (15-ounce) pinto beans, drained

1 large jalapeño pepper, chopped

Tortilla chips

1. Preheat oven to 350 degrees.
2. Coat a 9x13-inch baking pan with non-stick cooking spray.
3. In a large bowl, toss chicken with taco seasoning; add peppers, corn, beans and jalapeño pepper. Pour into baking pan.
4. Bake for 45 minutes; stir halfway through.
5. Serve with chips.

HINT: Can be served with corn or flour tortillas instead of the chips for a healthier dish. Also, the casserole can be made up to one day in advance and stored in the refrigerator, or up to two months in the freezer.

ITALIAN CHICKEN ON THE STOVE

My family and friends had a lot of nice things to say about the recipes they tested for this book. My friend Adina Klim wrote this note regarding this recipe: "Very quick, easy and tasty—a good one."

| Prep time: 3 min. | Cook time: 40 min. | Quantity: 4 servings |

3 tablespoons olive oil

4 boneless, skinless chicken breast halves

Italian seasoning

1 can (14-ounce) diced tomatoes

1 can (14-ounce) chicken broth

1 package (5-ounce) dry tomato soup mix

½ cup uncooked rice

1. In a large skillet, warm oil over medium high. Generously sprinkle both sides of chicken with Italian seasoning and place in skillet. Brown both sides of chicken, about 4 minutes per side.

2. In a medium bowl, combine tomatoes, chicken broth, soup mix and rice. Pour on top of chicken; bring to a boil. Cover pan tightly and reduce heat to medium-low.

3. Simmer mixture for 30 minutes, stirring once in middle of cooking. Make sure all liquid is absorbed and rice is tender.

4. Serve with a salad.

HINT: This dish works well re-warmed the next day.

L.Z.'S ENCHILADA CASSEROLE

Prep time: 15 min.   Bake time: 325°/30 min.   Quantity: 6-8 servings

1 can (28-ounce) mild enchilada sauce

8 corn tortillas (6-inch)

2 cups _cooked_ chicken, shredded

1½ cups Monterey Jack cheese, grated

1 bunch green onions, chopped

1 container (8-ounce) plain yogurt

1. Preheat oven to 325 degrees.
2. In a shallow bowl, pour 1 cup enchilada sauce.
3. Dip 4 tortillas in sauce and place in bottom of 9x13-inch baking pan coated with non-stick cooking spray.
4. Sprinkle tortillas with chicken, cheese, and onions.
5. Dip remaining 4 tortillas in the same enchilada sauce and place on top of chicken/cheese/onion mixture.
6. In the same shallow bowl, combine remaining enchilada sauce and yogurt; whisk.
7. Pour over top of casserole making sure to moisten all the tortillas with sauce.
8. Bake for 30 minutes. Remove from oven and let rest for 5 minutes before serving.

HINT: Serve with a green salad!

CHICKEN PIZZA Featured on the cover

So easy and yet so sophisticated. The family will love this treat.

| Prep time: 5 min. | Bake time: 425°/5-10 min. | Quantity: 4 servings |

3 tablespoons olive oil (divided)

1 large yellow, green or red pepper, sliced thinly

4 pita breads left whole *(trad jies shells)*

Garlic salt

2-3 medium tomatoes, sliced

½ pound **cooked** chicken breast, cut into ¼-inch slices

8 black olives, pitted, sliced

Hot pepper flakes (optional) *No*

1¼ cups mozzarella cheese, grated

1. Preheat oven to 425 degrees.
2. In a medium skillet, warm 1½ tablespoons olive oil over medium-high heat. Sauté pepper in skillet for 5 minutes; stir frequently; remove from heat.
3. Rub 1½ tablespoons olive oil over pitas; sprinkle both sides with garlic salt.
4. Place pitas on cookie sheet and top with tomato slices, chicken, olives, red pepper flakes and peppers; sprinkle with mozzarella cheese.
5. Bake for 5-10 minutes or until cheese is melted and bottom of pitas are crispy.
6. Serve.

HINT: For the greens lover in the family, remove pitas from oven and top with torn pieces of spinach before serving. You can serve this pizza with a side of pizza sauce for dipping. For a more sophisticated taste, sprinkle with Gorgonzola cheese and a few fresh herbs in place of the mozzarella cheese.

Barb and Tim Mansfield are good friends of our family. They tested this recipe, along with many others for this book. They used to own and operate a fabulous restaurant 'Out East' many years ago. Their sophisticated and helpful suggestions for the recipes have been invaluable to me—thank you!

One Dish Main Dish

AUTUMN CHICKEN

Great dish for the fall.

| Prep time: 3 min. | Cook time: 30 min. | Quantity: 4 servings |

2 tablespoons vegetable oil

4 boneless, skinless chicken breast halves

1 cup chicken broth

2 teaspoons Italian seasoning

1 large sweet potato, cut in ¼-inch discs

1 cup frozen green beans

Salt and pepper to taste

1. In a large skillet, warm oil over medium heat. Cook chicken breasts 8 minutes per side or until juices run clear.
2. Add broth, Italian seasoning and vegetables to skillet; bring to a boil and reduce heat to low.
3. Cover and simmer for 20 minutes or until vegetables are tender.
4. Serve.

HINT: My friend, Patti Nakfoor, is an emergency room doctor. Her husband and two sons are very active and are always going places. To test this recipe she threw all of the ingredients into a crockpot and cooked it at work. It turned out great, and the whole department loved the dish. I never thought of doing this but I'm glad Patti did—I hope you enjoy the dish.

BRUISER BEEF & BROCCOLI

The perfect protein dinner for your little b-ball player.

| Prep time: 10 min. | Cook time: 20 min. | Quantity: 4 servings |

2 tablespoons vegetable oil

¾-1 pound beef sirloin steak, cut into strips

1 large clove garlic, crushed*

1 medium onion, chopped

1 can (10¾-ounce) cream of chicken or mushroom soup

1 cup water

1½ tablespoons soy sauce

1 head broccoli, chopped

1. In a large skillet, warm oil over medium-high heat. Cook beef together **with garlic** until beef is browned, about 4-5 minutes.
2. Add onions to skillet and cook another 5 minutes; stir occasionally.
3. Add soup, water and soy sauce. Bring to a boil and reduce heat to low; add broccoli. Cover and simmer 5 minutes or until vegetables are tender.

HINT: Serve with rice, pasta or couscous.

*Use chopped or minced ready to use garlic in the jar for convenience.

One Dish Main Dish

PEPPER STEAK STIR FRY

Just make the instant rice while cooking the stir-fry and you will have a meal in 30 minutes. This recipe is very quick; the key is to use high heat to sear in the flavor.

Prep time: 10 min.   Marinate time: 1-12 hrs.   Cook time: 20 min.   Quantity: approx. 6 servings

1 pound top round beef, cut into ⅛-inch strips

1 tablespoon vegetable oil

1 cup green onion, thinly sliced

1 green pepper, chopped

1 red pepper, chopped

2 stalks celery, thinly sliced

1 can (8-ounce) sliced water chestnuts, drained reserving juices

1 can (4-ounce) sliced mushrooms, drained reserving juices

1 tablespoon cornstarch

Marinade

2 tablespoons soy sauce

2 tablespoons lemon juice

½ teaspoon ground ginger

¼ teaspoon garlic powder

⅛ teaspoon pepper

1. In a small bowl combine marinade ingredients; whisk.
2. Place beef strips in a non-reactive container (i.e. plastic); add the marinade to cover beef strips. Can be refrigerated for 1-12 hours in advance.
3. In a large skillet, warm oil over medium-high heat.
4. Remove beef from marinade; reserve marinade. Cook beef in skillet over high heat until browned and any remaining liquid evaporates, about 8 minutes.
5. Add vegetables to skillet; cover pan and cook until vegetables are cooked through but still cisp-tender, about 5 minutes.
6. In a small bowl, combine cornstarch, reserved juices from chestnuts, mushrooms and remaining reserved marinade; whisk. Reduce heat to medium-low and add to vegetable/beef mixture. Bring to a simmer and cook until thickened, about 5 minutes.
7. Serve!

HINT: Great with rice.

One Dish Main Dish

QUICK MAC CASSEROLE

This recipe is simple and will please everyone.

Prep time: 10 min.   Bake time: 350°/15-20 min.   Quantity: 6-8 servings

1 package (7.5-ounce) macaroni and cheese dinner

1 pound ground beef

1 stalk celery, sliced

½ green pepper, chopped

1 medium onion, chopped

2 cups frozen whole kernel corn

1 can (6-ounce) tomato paste

1 cup water

1 teaspoon salt

¼ teaspoon black pepper

1. Preheat oven to 350 degrees.
2. Coat a 9x13-inch baking pan with non-stick cooking spray.
3. Prepare macaroni and cheese dinner as directed on package.
4. While macaroni is cooking, combine ground meat, celery, green pepper and onion in large skillet over medium-high heat. Cook until tender and meat is browned, about 10 minutes.
5. Add corn, tomato paste, water, salt and pepper to the skillet; mix well.
6. Add prepared macaroni and cheese dinner to the skillet; mix well.
7. Pour skillet contents into baking pan. Cover and bake 15-20 minutes.
8. Serve.

HINT: Great to prepare ahead of time, freeze and re-heat in oven or microwave.

MACBURGER MEAL

This is a rich and satisfying meal that is quick and quite a child pleaser. Balance the richness of this meal with a fresh fruit salad.

Prep time: 2 min.   Cook time: 18 min.   Quantity: 4-6 servings

1-1¼ pounds ground meat, turkey or beef

2¾ cups water

⅓ cup ketchup

2 teaspoons onion powder

½ teaspoon salt

8 ounces elbow pasta, uncooked

12 ounces Velveeta®, cut up

1. In a large skillet, brown meat over medium-high heat, about 8 minutes; drain.
2. Add water, ketchup, onion powder and salt; bring to a boil; add pasta; stir to combine.
3. Reduce to medium-low and cover; simmer for 12 minutes.
4. Remove from heat and add cheese; stir until melted, about 1-2 minutes.
5. Serve.

QUICK PLAYERS PIE

An excellent alternative to meat pie. The vegetable protein mix does an excellent job of adding great flavor and texture to the dish. I always make two pies; serve one and freeze the other.

| Prep time: 10 min. | Bake time: 350°/325°/20 min. total | Quantity: 2 pies |

1 bag (12-ounce) frozen vegetable protein mix, thawed

½ cup seasoned breadcrumbs

1 medium onion, finely chopped

¼ teaspoon garlic powder

1 egg, slightly beaten

2 tablespoons water

1 tablespoon Worcestershire sauce

¼ teaspoon black pepper

¼ teaspoon salt

2½ cups prepared mashed potatoes (instant works great!)

2 cups sharp cheddar cheese, grated

2 cups frozen mixed vegetables

1. Preheat oven to 350 degrees.
2. Coat two 9-inch pie pans with non-stick cooking spray.
3. In a large bowl, place veggie protein mix, breadcrumbs, onion, garlic powder, egg, water, Worcestershire sauce, black pepper, and salt; mix with hands until well blended.
4. Press mixture over bottom and up sides of two 9-inch pie pans; form a shell.
5. Bake 10 minutes. Remove from oven; set aside.
6. Reduce oven to 325 degrees.
7. In the same large bowl, combine potatoes, cheese, frozen veggies; spoon into vegetable protein shell.
8. Bake until heated thoroughly and cheese begins to melt, about 10-15 minutes.
9. Serve.

*HINT: Tom and Linda Dufelmeier are neighbors who have been lucky and not so lucky enough to try many of my surprises and duds when working on this cookbook. They were part of the test team that made this recipe. They ate the first pie themselves, and gave the second to four college girls who consumed the pie in minutes (you know those starving college students). They **LOVED** it.*

One Dish Main Dish

QUICK TUNA AND NOODLES

After testing a lot of recipes for a tuna noodle dish, I found this recipe was the easiest and had the best flavor as well. This is one of those dishes that some people consider 'comfort food'.

Prep time: 5 min.   Cook time: 15 min.   Quantity: 4 servings

2½ cups water

8 ounces wide egg noodles, uncooked

12 ounces prepared cheese product, cut into ½-inch cubes (Velveeta® makes a good one)

1 package (16-ounce) frozen vegetables, (peas and carrots mix works well)

1 can (6-ounce) tuna, drained and flaked

½ cup water

½ teaspoon salt

¼ teaspoon black pepper

1. In a large skillet, bring 2½ cups of water to a boil. Reduce heat to medium-low and add noodles. Cover and simmer for 8 minutes or until noodles are tender; stir occasionally.

2. Add cheese, vegetables, tuna, ½ cup of water, salt and pepper to skillet; stir until cheese is melted.

3. Cover and cook for 3 minutes; serve.

PASS THE PASTA

Pasta is the perfect carbohydrate for a multitude of toppings. Most recipes in this chapter are designed so that when you put the pasta water on the stove to boil, you can do the remainder of the preparation – a very effective use of your precious time. When the pasta is done you'll be ready to serve the meal.

There are many options in this chapter to satisfy everybody's tastes. Remember to check out the selection of sauces at the end of the chapter as well!

SALSA CORN PASTA

Even though I am Italian and love a lot of dishes with tomato sauce, I never thought of putting salsa on pasta until my son mentioned the idea when I was testing dishes for this cookbook. I ran out of ingredients when preparing a dish and he suggested salsa, beans and onions. We ended up with this dish which is now a standard on our dinner menu!

Prep time: 5 min.	Cook time: 20 min.	Quantity: 4-6 servings

1 pound pasta, any style

1 can black beans, drained

1-2 cups corn, frozen (thawed)

2 cups salsa (your choice of spiciness)

1 bunch green onions, chopped

½ teaspoon chili powder

1 large avocado, peeled and cut into large 2-inch chunks

Sour cream

1. While boiling water for pasta, combine in a large serving bowl beans, corn, salsa, green onions and chili powder.
2. Drain pasta and transfer into serving bowl with other ingredients; toss well. Gently toss in avocado and serve with a dollop of sour cream.

HINT: Excellent hot, warm or cold!

SUMMER CHOP PASTA

A light summer meal—this can be prepared with the vinaigrette dressing given on the next page or with a good quality store-bought vinaigrette. Very fast, very easy and very good. Did I mention that it's very good for you, too!

Prep time: 5 min.	Cook time: 20 min.	Quantity: 4 servings

1 pound pasta, your choice

1 medium tomato, chopped

1 bunch green onions, chopped

2 radishes, chopped

2 carrots, peeled and chopped

1 green pepper, chopped

1 cup corn, frozen (thawed)

1. While boiling water for pasta, chop all the vegetables.
2. In a medium bowl, combine tomato, green onions and radishes.
3. Prepare dressing (see next page).
4. In bottom of colander (that you plan to drain pasta in) combine carrots, green pepper and corn.
5. Drain pasta directly over carrots, green peppers and corn; place in serving bowl. Add chopped tomato, scallions and radishes to pasta; toss well.
6. Drizzle with dressing and serve warm or cold.

CHOP SALAD VINAIGRETTE

½ cup olive oil

¼ cup lemon juice

1 tablespoon Dijon mustard

1 teaspoon oregano

1 teaspoon salt

¾ teaspoon pepper

1 large garlic clove, crushed*

1. Combine all ingredients in a medium bowl; whisk well.
2. Set aside until pasta is ready.

HINT: Keeps well in refrigerator up to 2 weeks.

*Use chopped or minced ready to use garlic in the jar for convenience.

CAESAR SALAD PASTA

An excellent pasta dish that can be served hot or cold. The Caesar salad dressing really adds zest to this salad.

| Prep time: 5 min. | Cook time: 20 min. | Quantity: 4-6 servings |

1 pound pasta, your choice

½ cup mayonnaise

¼ cup plain yogurt

½ - 1 cup Caesar salad dressing

2 **cooked** chicken breast halves, sliced

Romaine lettuce

1 large tomato, sliced

¼ red onion sliced

1. While boiling water for pasta, combine in a small bowl mayonnaise, yogurt and Caesar dressing; whisk.
2. Drain pasta; place in serving bowl; toss with dressing and chicken.
3. Serve on bed of lettuce; dress with tomato and red onion.

CHICKEN PASTA SAUTÉ

No need to wrap the leftovers—there won't be any!

Prep time: 5 min.   Cook time: 20 min.   Quantity: 4 servings

2 **_cooked_** boneless, skinless chicken breast halves, thinly sliced

½ package (1.25-ounce) fajita seasoning mix (2 tablespoons)

½ cup red pepper, chopped

3 tablespoons water

½ pound pasta, any kind

¼ cup mayonnaise

2 tablespoons ranch dressing

2 tablespoons Italian dressing

1. While boiling water for pasta, combine in a medium bowl fajita seasoning mix, red pepper and water; add chicken and toss to coat.
2. In a large pan over high heat, sear chicken mixture for 3 minutes; set aside.
3. In a large serving bowl, combine mayonnaise, ranch and Italian dressing.
4. Drain pasta, reserving ½ cup water.
5. Toss pasta in serving bowl with seared chicken, dressing mixture and reserved pasta water.
6. Serve hot.

HINT: For color and taste variations, try tossing pasta with ¼ cup of grated carrots, ½ cup of chopped green pepper or adding some frozen vegetable to the pasta for the last 3 minutes of cook time.

ROTINI MEXICALI

Any kind of fun shaped pasta is perfect with this turkey/vegetarian sauce. It has a Mexican flair!

Prep time: 10 min.   Cook time: 20 min.   Quantity: 4 servings

½ pound turkey breakfast sausage, removed from casings

1 teaspoon chili powder

½ teaspoon ground cumin

1 can (28-ounce) crushed tomatoes

1 teaspoon sugar

1 pound pasta (any kind of fun shape)

1 cup Monterey Jack cheese, grated

3 tablespoons jalapeño slices, chopped (optional)

1 large avocado, sliced

1. While boiling water for pasta, sauté sausage in a large skillet over medium-high heat. Cook until no longer pink. Break up meat with wooden spoon.
2. Add chili powder and cumin to meat and cook for 30 seconds (the mixture will be dry).
3. Add tomatoes and sugar to meat; bring to a boil and reduce heat to low. Cover and simmer for 15 minutes; stir occasionally.
4. Toss cooked and drained pasta with sauce, Monterey jack cheese, jalapeño slices and avocado.
5. Serve hot.

SPRING GREEN PASTA

This dish is fresh and tasty. Great on a spring day when you get home from work and would rather spend time outside than in the kitchen. The fresh parsley really adds a special touch.

Prep time: none	Cook time: 20 min.	Quantity: 4 servings

1 pound pasta (thick meaty kind like linguine or rigatoni)

¾ cup mayonnaise

3 tablespoons Dijon mustard

2 tablespoons _fresh_ parsley, chopped

½ teaspoon thyme

¼ teaspoon salt

½ pound ham, diced

1 cup corn, frozen (thawed)

1 bunch green onions, chopped

1. While boiling water for pasta, combine in a medium bowl mayonnaise, Dijon mustard, parsley, thyme and salt; whisk. Add ham, corn and scallions to Dijon dressing.
2. Drain pasta, reserving ½ cup water. Place pasta in large serving bowl; toss with Dijon dressing and reserved pasta water.
3. Serve warm or cold.

BETTER BUTTERED NOODLES

This recipe makes the "buttered noodle dish" more palatable for the whole family. Great by itself or as a side dish to chicken or meat.

| Prep time: 5 min. | Cook time: 20 min. | Quantity: 4 servings |

1 pound rigatoni

4 tablespoons butter

⅛-¼ teaspoon nutmeg

½ cup Parmesan cheese, grated

Black pepper

1. Cook rigatoni to desired tenderness.
2. Drain rigatoni, reserving ½ cup of water. Place in pasta bowl and toss with butter, nutmeg, cheese and reserved pasta water.
3. Serve hot.

EASY-CHEESY PASTA SALAD

Easy, cheesy, and fun for a BBQ.

Prep time: 5 min.	Cook time: 20 min.	Refrigeration time: 1-2 hours	Quantity: 4-6 servings

¾ cup mayonnaise

½ cup Molly McButter® natural cheese flavor sprinkles

¼ cup pickle relish

12 ounces pasta

2 cups frozen peas, cooked

1 red bell pepper, chopped

Salt to taste

1. While boiling water for pasta, combine in a small bowl mayonnaise, cheese sprinkles and relish.
2. Drain pasta; rinse in cold water and drain well. Place in large bowl; add peas, red pepper and mayonnaise mixture to pasta; mix thoroughly.
3. Cover and refrigerate 1-2 hours before serving.
4. Keeps up to 5 days in refrigerator.

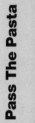

Pass The Pasta

KIDS LOVE THIS PASTA

Kids love this pasta!

| Prep time: 5 min. | Cook time: 20 min. | Quantity: 4-6 servings |

1 pound pasta (any kind of fun shape)

1 head of broccoli, chopped

1 jar (16-ounce) processed cheese product (Velveeta® makes a good one)

⅛ teaspoon garlic salt

1. While boiling water for pasta, chop broccoli.
2. During the last 3 minutes of cook time for the pasta, add the broccoli to the pasta pot.
3. Drain pasta and broccoli; transfer immediately to serving bowl.
4. Add cheese and garlic salt; toss until cheese coats pasta.
5. Serve immediately.

CAESAR WITH BOWTIES

Easy is the name of the game here. I used to make my own Caesar salad dressing for this recipe but the store-bought kind works great and is a perfect time saver!

| Prep time: 5 min. | Cook time: 20 min. | Quantity: 4-6 servings |

½ cup Caesar salad dressing

1 can (15-ounce) tomato puree

1 pound **cooked** bowtie pasta

¼ cup **fresh** parsley, chopped

¼ cup red onion, thinly sliced

½ cup cherry tomatoes, halved

1. While boiling water for pasta, combine in a medium bowl the Caesar dressing and tomato puree; whisk.
2. Drain pasta and place in serving bowl.
3. Toss pasta with dressing mixture, parsley, onion and cherry tomatoes.
4. Serve warm, room temperature or cold.

HINT: Serve with fresh grated Parmesan cheese and a green salad.

SUPERB LINGUINE

This dish is so light and creamy—your family will think that you slaved over it all day. It really is superb!

| Prep time: 5 min. | Cook time: 20 min. | Quantity: 4-6 servings |

1 pound linguine

4 cups broccoli florets, fresh or frozen

1 cup ham, chopped

½ cup mayonnaise (low-fat works well)

¼ cup Parmesan cheese, grated

¼ cup whole milk

½ teaspoon garlic powder

½ teaspoon basil

1. While boiling water for pasta, chop broccoli.
2. During the last 3 minutes of cooking time for the pasta, add the broccoli to the pasta water.
3. Drain the pasta and broccoli; toss in a big bowl with remaining ingredients.
4. Serve immediately or serve cold.

HINT: In place of broccoli try frozen peas, corn, or vegetable blend, as an alternative.

VEGGIE-LIGHT FETTUCCINE

The smoked turkey is the key to this light and flavorful dish.

Prep time: 5 min.　Cook time: 20 min.　Quantity: 4-6 servings

1 pound fettuccine

1¾ cups _skim_ milk

1 package (8-ounce) _light_ cream cheese, cubed

½ cup green onion, chopped

1 teaspoon Italian seasoning

¼ teaspoon garlic powder

1 cup cooked smoked turkey breast meat, cubed (deli style works fine)

½ cup Parmesan cheese

1 cup _each_: broccoli florets, carrot slices and zucchini slices

1. While boiling water for pasta, combine in a microwaveable bowl milk, cream cheese, onions and seasonings.
2. Microwave on high for 2-3 minutes. Stir every minute until it has a smooth consistency and is warmed through.
3. Add turkey and Parmesan cheese to cream sauce; stir to combine. Set cream sauce aside.
4. During last 3 minutes of cooking time for the pasta, add broccoli, carrots and zucchini to the pasta pot.
5. Drain pasta and vegetables, place in serving bowl and toss with sauce. Wait 2 minutes before serving. Toss again and serve.

HINT: Very rich and full of veggies! You will never miss the fat!

SHELLS AND CHEESE

In thirty-five minutes you can have a yummy meal on the table.

Prep time: 10 min.	Cook time: 25 min.	Quantity: 4 servings

12 ounces medium size pasta shells

1 tablespoon oil (olive or vegetable)

½ green pepper, diced

1 small onion, diced

1 clove garlic, crushed*

1½ cups prepared spaghetti sauce

1 cup water

½ teaspoon oregano

1 tablespoon dried parsley

4 ounces American cheese cut into 1-inch cubes

1. While boiling water for pasta, warm oil in large skillet over medium heat. Sauté green pepper, onion and garlic in skillet, until crisp and browned about 8-10 minutes.
2. Add sauce, water, oregano and parsley to skillet and simmer 5 minutes.
3. Remove from heat and stir in cheese cubes; pour over cooked and drained pasta.
4. Serve.

Use chopped or minced ready to use garlic in the jar for convenience.

SPINACH FETA MOSTACCIOLI

Great when served on the deck on a hot summer evening when the kids are actually home for dinner!

Prep time: 5 min.   Cook time: 20 min.   Quantity: 4-6 servings

1 pound pasta (your choice)

3 large tomatoes, chopped

1 package (10-ounce) frozen chopped spinach, thawed and well drained

1 bunch green onions, chopped

8 ounces Feta cheese, crumbled

4 tablespoons olive oil

Salt and pepper

1. While boiling water for pasta, combine tomatoes, spinach, green onions, Feta cheese and olive oil in medium bowl.

2. Drain pasta, reserving ½ cup water. Place pasta in large serving bowl. Toss pasta with oil, tomatoes, spinach, onions, Feta cheese and reserved pasta water; salt and pepper to taste.

3. Serve hot or room temperature.

HINT: Thaw spinach in microwave for quick results. As an alternative, sprinkle basil or oregano over tomatoes before tossing all together.

FAST SKILLET PASTA

Great to serve as a side dish or as a main dish. Simple but complete in flavor!

| Prep time: 5 min. | Cook time: 15 min. | Quantity: 4 servings |

2 tablespoons olive oil

2 bunches green onion, chopped

¼ large green pepper, chopped

2½ cups water

2 chicken bouillon cubes

½ teaspoon garlic powder

1 cup orzo pasta* (the pasta shaped like rice)

1. In a medium skillet, warm olive oil over medium heat. Sauté onion and green pepper until tender, about 5 minutes.
2. Add water, bouillon cubes and garlic powder to skillet; bring to boil. Add uncooked pasta* to skillet and return to a boil. Reduce heat and simmer.
3. Cover and cook for 10 minutes or until pasta is tender.
4. Serve!

Very small pasta works best like orzo, acine di pepe, or stars.

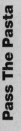

QUICK HOT PASTA SALAD

Great for the evenings when you can add a little bit of everything from the vegetable drawer for a meal.

Prep time: 5 min.   Cook time: 20 min.   Quantity: 2-4 servings

8 ounces pasta (any kind)

½ cup _each_ vegetable: zucchini, broccoli, cauliflower and onion; chopped

2 tablespoons olive oil

⅓ cup creamy Italian dressing

3-4 tablespoons grated Parmesan cheese

1. While boiling water for pasta, chop the vegetables.
2. About 3 minutes before the pasta is done add the vegetables to the pasta water.
3. Drain pasta and vegetables. In serving bowl, toss pasta and vegetables with olive oil, creamy Italian dressing, and cheese.
4. Voila! Serve.

PEAS CHEESE AND PASTA BAKE

A make ahead meal!

Prep time: 5 min.	Bake time: 350°/35 min.	Quantity: 6-8 servings

1 pound pasta (any kind of fun shape)

1 pound cottage cheese

2 cups grated mozzarella cheese

2 cups frozen peas

¼ cup grated Parmesan cheese

3 large eggs, slightly beaten

½ teaspoon garlic powder (optional)

½ teaspoon salt

½ teaspoon pepper

1 jar (28-ounce) spaghetti sauce, any flavor

1. Preheat oven to 350 degrees.
2. While boiling water for pasta, combine in medium bowl cottage cheese, mozzarella cheese, peas, Parmesan cheese, eggs, garlic powder, salt and pepper; mix well.
3. Drain pasta and return to cooking pot. Toss pasta with whole jar of spaghetti sauce.
4. Spray a 2½-quart casserole dish with non-stick cooking spray. Layer in casserole dish ½ pasta and then ½ cheese mixture.
5. Cover with remaining pasta and remaining cheese mixture.
6. You can cover and refrigerate for up to 2 days at this point. Bake for 35 minutes or until hot and bubbly.
7. Serve.

HINT: For those who like a saucy dish, you may want to add 1 cup of extra sauce.

SAUSAGE AND MOZZARELLA LASAGNA

This takes a little more time to put together, but it's worth the effort. The whole family will love the dish.

Prep time: 30 min.   Bake time: 375°/35 min.   Quantity: 8 servings

1 pound Italian sausage, casings removed, **browned and crumbled**

2 jars (28-ounce each) pasta sauce

1 container (15-ounce) ricotta cheese

1 large egg

¼ cup Parmesan cheese, grated

1 tablespoon parsley flakes

Pinch of salt

½ teaspoon pepper

1 box (9-ounce) no-boil lasagna pasta sheets (may say 'oven ready'), approx. 16 sheets

3 cups mozzarella cheese, grated

1. Preheat oven to 375 degrees.
2. In a large bowl, combine ricotta cheese, egg, Parmesan cheese, parsley, salt and pepper; mix well and set aside.
3. Spray a 9x13-inch baking pan with non-stick cooking spray and follow these easy steps:
   - Pour 1 cup of sauce in bottom of baking pan; spread evenly.
   - Lay 4 sheets of lasagna noodles over top of sauce in a single layer.
   - Cover with 1 cup of sauce and ½ of the sausage.
   - Take ¼ of ricotta mixture and distribute evenly over sauce by spoonfuls (even out the lumps).
   - Sprinkle ½ cup of mozzarella cheese over top of ricotta cheese.
4. Repeat these steps three more times. Make sure top layer is covered with remaining sauce and mozzarella.* Cover dish with foil, making sure foil does not touch top layer of lasagna.
5. Bake for 25 minutes, remove foil and bake 10 minutes longer or until top is bubbling and golden.
6. Let stand 5 minutes before serving.

*HINT: The key to baking with the 'oven ready' lasagna is to make sure all the edges are covered with sauce so the pasta sheets don't dry out and become hard while baking.

CHICKEN AND PASTA

A great dinner—just add the salad!

Prep time: 5 min.	Cook time: 20 min.	Quantity: 3-4 servings

8 ounces pasta (any kind)

4 boneless, skinless chicken breast halves

2 tablespoons vegetable oil

1 package (.7-ounce) dry Italian salad dressing mix (Good Seasons® makes a good one)

1 teaspoon red wine vinegar

2 tablespoons butter

2 tablespoons water

1. While boiling water for pasta, warm oil in a large ***non-stick*** skillet over medium heat.

2. Reserve 2 teaspoons Italian seasoning mix; set aside. Coat both sides of chicken with remaining seasoning mix.

3. Cook chicken in skillet, approximately 8 minutes per side or until juices run clear when cut through thickest part. Remove chicken to serving platter and keep warm.

4. Add vinegar, butter and water to skillet. Stir until butter melts, about 10 seconds; set aside.

5. Drain pasta, reserving ½ cup water. Place pasta in large serving bowl and toss to coat with butter sauce from step 4, the reserved seasoning mix and reserved pasta water.

6. Place chicken on top of pasta and serve.

EASY PEANUT SAUCE

*If you haven't tried peanut sauce on pasta or chicken, you are really missing out! The ingredients in this recipe combine together quickly and easily to make **one** outstanding flavor!*

| Prep time: 3 min. | Microwave time: 2 min. | Quantity: approx. 1¼ cups sauce |

½ cup peanut butter, creamy

¼ teaspoon red pepper flakes

1 tablespoon soy sauce

1 large garlic clove, crushed*

1 teaspoon curry powder

¾ cup chicken broth

1. Combine all ingredients in a medium microwaveable bowl; whisk lightly.
2. Cover with plastic wrap lightly and microwave on high 1-2 minutes or until smooth and slightly thick. If you prefer a thinner sauce, add a little more chicken broth.

HINT: Great sauce for about 12 ounces of pasta, or use as a dipping sauce for grilled chicken strips.

*Use chopped or minced ready to use garlic in the jar for convenience.

ROCKIN' SOCKIN' SOCCER SAUCE

I was planning to make chili one evening for my son and his friend before their soccer game when I realized the friend would not eat beans, only pasta. I came up with this sauce and served it over elbow macaroni. It was a big hit and I let the boys name it!

Prep time: 5 min.	Cook time: 15-30 min.	Quantity: a large quantity

3 pounds ground meat

1 large onion, chopped

3 large garlic cloves, crushed*

2 cans (32-ounce each) tomato sauce

¼ cup chili powder

1 tablespoon ground cumin

1. Brown meat in big pot and drain off any obvious fat.
2. Add onion and garlic to ground meat and cook until onion is soft, about 5 minutes.
3. Add tomato sauce, chili powder and ground cumin.
4. This can simmer on stove for as little as 15 minutes or as long as 2 hours. The flavor will vary depending on the length of time on the stove.

HINT: This makes a lot and it freezes beautifully. I freeze the sauce in multiple containers and just pull out what I need for a fast dinner.

*Use chopped or minced ready to use garlic in the jar for convenience.

WHITE CLAM SAUCE

How can something so good be this easy?!

Prep time: 5 min.	Cook time: 5 min.	Quantity: 2-4 servings

3 tablespoons butter

1 large garlic clove, crushed*

1 tablespoon all-purpose flour

2 cans whole minced clams

¼ cup *fresh* parsley, chopped

¾ teaspoon dried basil

1⅓ cups half and half

Salt to taste

1. In a medium skillet over medium heat, melt butter. Sauté garlic in butter for 1 minute; whisk in flour.
2. Reduce heat to low; add clams, parsley, basil and half and half. Cover and simmer on low for 3-4 minutes; stir frequently.

HINT: Makes enough sauce for about 12 ounces of linguine. Remember to reserve about ½ cup water before draining pasta. Use reserved water to moisten the pasta when tossing with the sauce.

*Use chopped or minced ready to use garlic in the jar for convenience.

Pass The Pasta

PEANUT SAUCE FOR PASTA

This recipe is very versatile and can be used with most any pasta. See 'HINT' below for options.

Prep time: 5 min.	Cook time: none	Quantity: approx. 1½ cups

½ cup peanut butter, creamy

1 cup very hot water

1 large garlic clove, crushed*

1½ tablespoons soy sauce

1 teaspoon sesame oil

1. Mix everything together and toss with cooked pasta (approx. 12 ounces).

HINT: Add steamed vegetables such as peas, broccoli, carrots, or water chestnuts to the tossed pasta for great texture and flavor. Hot pepper flakes can be added for the hot tongue in the family.

*Use chopped or minced ready to use garlic in the jar for convenience.

FAMILY MEALS

No matter how busy you are, there needs to be time when the whole family re-groups and has a meal together, whether it is family meeting night or Sunday dinner. A family meal is a necessity so that you can count heads and make sure you didn't forget to pick someone up after the last soccer match or today's group piano lesson.

This chapter covers all kinds of recipes that take longer than 30 minutes but are still easy and fun to make. Most recipes do not require a lot of maintenance or time to prepare. They are just those good 'ole Sunday dinner recipes that your Mom used to make, slightly modified for today's more convenient lifestyle. I hope you enjoy them as much as I do!

Check out the great marinades and breakfast dishes at the end of this chapter. You will just love them!

NEIGHBORHOOD CHICKEN

When you want to make a dish that 1. Freezes well __before__ baking, 2. Serves a lot of people at once, 3. Is suitable for a potluck or a family in need, 4. Freezes well __after__ baking, and 5. Is versatile with any other dish, this recipe is it. I have made this recipe a million times, (maybe not that many times), and have given it to many friends who have called me back with their thanks and their variation on the recipe. Some of those variations are listed below.

> Prep time: 5 min.　　Bake time: 350°/1½ hrs.　　Quantity: 8-10 servings

2 large chicken fryers (4-5 pounds each) cut up (_not_ boneless chicken breasts)

1 bottle (16-ounce) Russian salad dressing

2 packages (1.25-ounce each) dry onion soup mix

1 jar (18-ounce) apricot preserves

1. Preheat oven to 350 degrees.
2. Coat 2 large casserole dishes with non-stick cooking spray.
3. Place chicken in one layer in casserole dishes.
4. In a medium bowl, combine dressing, soup mix, and preserves; pour over chicken.
5. Cover and bake for 1 hour. Remove cover and bake an additional ½ hour.
6. Serve over rice, noodles, or couscous.

Optional Variations

Add chopped green pepper, mushrooms, zucchini, or olives at step 3. Garnish with cherry tomatoes before ready to serve.

> *HINT: You can use 'pick of the chick' already cut up or assorted thighs and drumsticks. You can remove the skin from the chicken if you prefer and still have a tender piece of meat when ready to serve! Whatever you do—do not use boneless/skinless chicken breasts in this recipe. You will end up with 'rubber chicken' instead of 'neighborhood chicken'.*

CHILI-BAKED CHICKEN

Great flavor with a crispy skin!

Prep time: 10 min.	Bake time: 375°/1 hr.	Quantity: 6-8 servings

4 tablespoons vegetable oil, divided

½ cup cornmeal

½ cup flour

2 teaspoons dried oregano

1 teaspoon salt

1½ teaspoons cumin

1 tablespoon chili powder

½ teaspoon cayenne pepper to taste

1 whole chicken, cut-up

⅓ cup buttermilk

1 large zip-top plastic bag

1. Preheat oven to 375 degrees.
2. Coat large baking dish with non-stick cooking spray.
3. Evenly spread 2 tablespoons of oil in bottom of baking dish.
4. Combine all dry ingredients in large zip-top plastic bag and shake up to combine; set aside.
5. Pour buttermilk in a large shallow bowl. Pat chicken dry with paper towels, then dip chicken in buttermilk; place in zip-top plastic bag with dry ingredients.
6. Shake zip-top bag until all pieces of chicken are coated, about 20 seconds (don't forget to close the bag tightly!).
7. Place coated chicken in baking dish and drizzle with remaining 2 tablespoons of oil. Bake uncovered for 1 hour. Turn chicken pieces over once or twice to make both sides crispy.
8. The chicken will be deep brown when finished.

STUFFED CHICKEN DINNER

A satisfying soft stuffing with a great Mexican flair.

| Prep time: 10 min. | Bake time: 375°/1 hr. | Quantity: 4 servings |

1 whole chicken, cut up

3 cups stuffing, any flavor

¾ cup chicken broth

2 tablespoons margarine

1 package (.87-ounce) chicken gravy mix

2 tablespoons fajita seasoning mix

1 cup cold water

1. Preheat oven to 375 degrees.
2. Coat large casserole dish with non-stick cooking spray.
3. Place chicken in casserole dish.
4. In a microwaveable bowl, combine stuffing, chicken broth and margarine; microwave for 1 minute and fluff with fork. Place prepared stuffing around chicken pieces.
5. In the same microwaveable bowl, combine chicken gravy mix, fajita seasoning mix and cold water; whisk; microwave for 1 minute. Pour over chicken and stuffing mixture.
6. Cover and bake for 45 minutes. Remove cover and bake 15 minutes longer.
7. Serve!

*HINT: You can use 4 skinless chicken breast halves **with bone** to reduce fat. Serve with steamed carrots and dinner rolls.*

KEEP A SECRET CHICKEN

I got this recipe from a friend who promised not to tell who she got it from. Don't tell anyone how you made this dish because they won't believe how easy it is to make.

Prep time: 5 min.   Bake time: 400°/35 min.   Quantity: 4 servings

4 boneless, skinless chicken breast halves

1 package (1.4-ounce) herb/vegetable soup mix

⅓ cup mayonnaise

¼ cup grated Parmesan cheese

2 tablespoons seasoned bread crumbs

1. Preheat oven to 400 degrees.
2. Coat large baking dish with non-stick cooking spray.
3. Place chicken in one layer in baking dish.
4. In a small bowl, combine soup mix, mayonnaise and cheese.
5. Top chicken with soup mix evenly and sprinkle with breadcrumbs. Cover and bake 35 minutes.
6. Serve.

HINT: If chicken is thicker than ½-inch bake until juices run clear when pierced.

CHICKEN TENDER AND QUICK

Melt in your mouth, creamy and tender!

| Prep time: 10 min. | Bake time: 350°/40 min. | Quantity: 4 servings |

4 boneless, skinless chicken breast halves

4 slices Swiss cheese

1 can (10.5-ounce) cream of chicken soup

½ cup water

1 stick butter or margarine

2 cups stuffing (any flavor)

1. Preheat oven to 350 degrees.
2. Coat a 9x13-inch baking pan with non-stick cooking spray.
3. Place chicken in pan; top each piece with one slice of Swiss cheese.
4. In a medium microwaveable bowl, mix the can of soup with water; pour over chicken.
5. In the same medium bowl, melt butter in microwave; add stuffing and mix with fork until combined. Place stuffing mixture around and on top of chicken.
6. Cover and bake for 20 minutes; remove covering and bake an additional 20 minutes.
7. Serve!

FAMILY PARTY CHICKEN

You may be surprised to see the bake time on this dish but you will be amazed with the finished product. An ultimately butter soft chicken dish with little effort. An outstanding dish for any occasion!

Prep time: 5 min.	Cook time: 300°/2 hrs.	Quantity: 4 servings

8 slices bacon

4 boneless, skinless chicken breasts halves

12 ounces sour cream

1 can (10.5-ounce) cream of mushroom or cream of potato soup

1. Preheat oven to 300 degrees.
2. Coat a 9x13-inch baking pan with non-stick cooking spray.
3. Wrap 2 slices of bacon around each piece of chicken; place in baking pan.
4. In a small bowl, mix sour cream with your choice of soup; pour over chicken breasts.
5. Cover and bake for 2 hours.
6. Serve.

HINT: This recipe makes a lot of gravy. You can serve the chicken over rice or egg noodles or you can increase the chicken to 6 breast halves and 12 bacon slices to feed more people with an average amount of gravy for each serving. Garnish with roasted red pepper slices for presentation and flavor!

QUICK-CHIK PARMESAN

This recipe is delicious, quick and simple. Everyone will love it.

Prep time: 10 min.	Bake time: 400°/30 min.	Quantity: 4 servings

4 boneless, skinless chicken breast halves

1 large egg, beaten

¾ cup seasoned breadcrumbs

1 jar (28-ounce) prepared spaghetti sauce

1 cup shredded mozzarella cheese

1. Preheat oven to 400 degrees.
2. Coat large baking dish with non-stick cooking spray.
3. Place beaten egg and breadcrumbs in two separate bowls.
4. Pat chicken breasts dry with paper towels; dip in egg and then in breadcrumbs.
5. Arrange chicken in bottom of baking dish in one layer.
6. Bake uncovered for 20 minutes; pour spaghetti sauce over chicken and cover with cheese. Bake covered 10 minutes more or when juices run clear.
7. Serve.

HINT: If the chicken breasts are thicker than ½-inch bake until juices run clear when pierced. Serve with pasta, couscous or rice, Italian bread and a salad.

EASTERN CROCKPOT CHICKEN

A delicious dish that is very economical. Chicken legs and thighs are always a good price at the grocery store and make this dish fantastic with little effort.

| Prep time: 10 min. | Crockpot time: 8 hrs. | Quantity: 4-6 servings |

1 large onion, chopped

Grated peel of 1 large orange (juice and reserve)

2 tablespoons Worcestershire sauce

2 tablespoons soy sauce

2 tablespoons Dijon mustard

1-2 large garlic cloves, crushed*

½ teaspoon salt

4 chicken drumsticks

4 chicken thighs

1 cup diced dried fruit, your choice (prunes, dates, apricots, cherries, raisins or cranberries)

1. Place onions in bottom of slow cooker.
2. In a large bowl, mix orange peel, reserved orange juice, Worcestershire sauce, soy sauce, mustard, garlic and salt. Add chicken and fruit; toss to coat.
3. Place chicken mixture in slow cooker and cook on low for 8 hours.

HINT: Serve with mashed potatoes and green peas. You can take the skin off the chicken leg and thighs without loosing any flavor.

*Use chopped or minced ready to use garlic in the jar for convenience.

CHEESE BAKED CHICKEN WRAPS

Creamy texture inside the wrap with great flavor throughout. Simple to put together.

Prep time: 12 min.   Bake time: 350°/30 min.   Quantity: 4-6 servings

1 package (8-ounce) cream cheese, softened

½ small onion, chopped

½ tablespoon garlic salt

1 can (4-ounce) green chilies, chopped

2-3 *cooked* boneless, skinless chicken breast halves, shredded

2 cups cheddar cheese, grated, divided

1 can (10-ounce) Rotell® (chopped tomato with jalapeño peppers)

½ cup milk

8 flour tortillas

1. Preheat oven to 350 degrees.
2. Coat a 9x13-inch baking pan with non-stick cooking spray.
3. In a small bowl, combine cream cheese, onion, garlic salt and ½ can of chilies; mix well.
4. Lay 8 tortillas out on counter; spread with cream cheese mixture. Top with chicken and 1 cup cheddar cheese; roll up and place in prepared pan.
5. In the same small bowl, combine tomatoes, milk and remaining chilies. Pour over tortillas and sprinkle with remaining 1 cup of cheddar cheese.
6. Bake uncovered for 30 minutes and serve.

NOTE: For a time saver, use 3-4 cans of white meat chicken in place of shredded chicken breast. This dish keeps well in the refrigerator up to 2 days after preparing.

LICKIN' CHICKIN' FINGERS

This is a great recipe for the chicken finger eater in the family. This recipe freezes very well before or after baking.

Prep time: 15 min.   Bake time: 350°/25 min.   Quantity: approx. 15 fingers

1 large egg, beaten

½ cup milk

1 teaspoon Dijon mustard

2-3 shakes hot sauce (such as Tabasco)

½ teaspoon garlic salt

⅛ teaspoon pepper

½ cup flour

2 cups cornflake crumbs

1½ pounds chicken breast tenders

4 tablespoons margarine, melted

1. Preheat oven to 350 degrees.
2. In a shallow bowl, combine egg, milk, mustard, hot pepper, garlic salt, and pepper; whisk in flour.
3. Place cornflake crumbs in another shallow bowl.
4. Dip chicken tenders in egg mixture and then roll in cornflake crumbs, coating completely.
5. Place on cookie sheet; drizzle with melted margarine.
6. Bake for 25 minutes or until chicken is cooked through and crispy on the outside.

HINT: You can dip in a honey mustard sauce bought from the store or combine ¼ cup each of honey, Dijon mustard and mayonnaise for a yummy dip. Try the Crazy Dipping Sauce recipe in the **AFTER SCHOOL SNACKS** *chapter for another great dip idea.*

HOT CHICKEN SALAD

I have used this recipe for so many years, it's become an old stand-by when I have some chicken left over from the night before and I don't want the kids to know I'm serving them leftovers for dinner.

Prep time: 10 min.   Bake time: 350°/25 min.   Quantity: 6-8 servings

8 ounces elbow or similar pasta, cooked until barely tender

1 can (10.5-ounce) cream of mushroom soup

½ cup mayonnaise

2 tablespoons soy sauce

2 tablespoons lemon juice

2 cups *cooked* chicken, cubed

1½ cups chopped celery

1 can (8-ounce) sliced water chestnuts, drained

1-2 bunches green onions

1 cup chow mein noodles

1. Preheat oven to 350 degrees.
2. Coat a 9x13-inch casserole dish with non-stick cooking spray.
3. While preparing to boil pasta, in large bowl, combine soup, mayonnaise, soy sauce and lemon juice; blend well.
4. In same large bowl add chicken, celery, water chestnuts, green onion and drained pasta; blend well.
5. Pour chicken/pasta mixture into prepared casserole dish and sprinkle with chow mein noodles.
6. Bake uncovered for 25 minutes or until warmed through.
7. Serve.

PIZZASTEAK

This is a delicious, easy way to serve red meat with a little fun and a great pizza flavor!

| Prep time: 10 min. | Cook time: 30 min. | Quantity: 3 servings |

3 tablespoons olive oil

3 large cloves garlic, crushed*

1 whole thin-cut sirloin steak, about 1 pound

3 tablespoons flour

1 can (15-ounce) puréed tomatoes

1 tablespoon dried basil

1 tablespoon dried oregano

1 tablespoon dried parsley

Salt and pepper to taste

1 tablespoon olive oil

1. In a large skillet, warm 3 tablespoons olive oil over medium heat; sauté garlic for 1 minute.
2. In the meantime, notch edges of meat with a sharp knife to prevent curling.
3. Place flour in shallow bowl; dredge steak lightly in flour.
4. Push garlic to sides of skillet and add steak.
5. Increase heat to medium-high and brown steak quickly, about 4 minutes per side. Remove meat from skillet and keep warm.
6. Reduce heat to medium and add the tomatoes, basil, oregano, and parsley to the skillet. Season with salt and pepper and simmer for 15 minutes; stir occasionally.
7. Add steak to skillet; drizzle steak with 1 tablespoon olive oil. Stir everything around and cover with lid; simmer on medium-low 10 minutes longer.
8. Serve immediately.

Use chopped or minced ready to use garlic in the jar for convenience.

FAMILY MEETING POT ROAST

The key to this fantastic recipe is the cut of meat. Do not substitute a different cut of meat. My friend, Jane, tested this recipe and used a really nice cut of meat—needless to say it turned out horrible, but when I heard about this I quickly went out and purchased all the ingredients with the specified cut of meat and brought it to her house. That evening Jane prepared the meal and the entire family called me on the phone to rave about the incredible meal that was served. It's all in the meat!!!

Prep time: 15 min.	Bake time: 325°/2 hrs. 45 min.	Quantity: 6 servings

3-4 pound *bottom round beef roast*

2 tablespoons flour

1 tablespoon olive oil

1½ cups water

¼ cup balsamic vinegar

½ teaspoon salt

¼ teaspoon black pepper

1 package (1.4-ounce) instant vegetable soup mix (Knorr® makes a good one)

1 large red onion, quartered

4 large baking potatoes, quartered (peeling is optional)

3 large carrots, cut in half (peeling is optional)

1. Preheat oven to 325 degrees.
2. Spray large roasting pan with non-stick cooking spray; place roast in pan.
3. In a medium bowl, combine flour, olive oil, water, vinegar and soup mix; whisk until flour and soup mix dissolve in liquid.
4. Pour over roast in pan and then place vegetables around the roast; salt and pepper to taste.
5. Cover and bake for 2 hours and 45 minutes or until tender.

HINT: Great served with steamed broccoli and crusty bread.

AMERICAN BEEF ROAST

A recipe that is quick to put together and tastes fantastic. This is an easy meal to serve when you need a good source of protein and you have a lot of mouths to feed on a Sunday afternoon.

Prep time: 5 min.   Bake time: 325°/3-4 hrs.   Quantity: 6-8 servings

3-4 pound sirloin tip or rump roast

3-4 large garlic cloves, crushed*

3-4 sprigs fresh Italian parsley

1 can (4-ounce) mushrooms, drained

1 package (.87-ounce) brown gravy mix

2-3 cups water

Salt and pepper to taste

1. Preheat oven to 325 degrees.
2. Spray large roasting pan with non-stick cooking spray.
3. Place meat in pan; toss garlic and parsley on top of the meat (no need to chop the parsley).
4. In a small bowl, whisk mushrooms, gravy mix and 1 cup of water; pour over roast. Salt and pepper the roast to taste.
5. Cover and cook for 3-4 hours or until meat is fork tender. Add an extra cup of water every hour to juices in pan (this will create rich mushroom gravy when ready to serve). Add an extra cup of water 15 minutes before serving for thinner gravy.
6. Serve.

HINT: During the last hour you can add peeled potatoes and carrots for a complete meal.

**Use chopped or minced ready to use garlic in the jar for convenience.*

CLASSIC WILLIAMS' POT ROAST

This recipe has been in the Williams family for years and has served three hungry boys who played sports like football, track, basketball, softball and baseball through the years! I feel privileged to put this wonderful recipe in this cookbook. Awesome flavor!

| Prep time: 5 min. | Roast time: 310°/3-4 hrs. | Quantity: 6 servings |

4 pound beef roast

1 medium onion, chopped

1 package (1-ounce) Au Jus Natural® style gravy mix

1 cup water

¼ cup ketchup

½ cup dry red wine

2 teaspoons Dijon mustard

1 teaspoon Worcestershire sauce

¼ teaspoon garlic powder

¼ teaspoon salt

⅛ teaspoon pepper

1. Preheat oven to 310 degrees (yes that is 310 degrees!).
2. Coat large baking pan with non-stick cooking spray.
3. Place roast in pan and cover with onion.
4. In a medium bowl, combine rest of ingredients; whisk until combined.
5. Pour over roast, cover and cook for 3-4 hours or until it is 'butter knife' tender.
6. Serve!

HINT: Serve with mashed potatoes and a green salad. Add peeled carrots in last hour of cooking for added sweetness to gravy.

HUNGARIAN BEEF

The caraway seeds really make this dish unique!

| Prep time: 10 min. | Crockpot time: High 5 hrs. or Low 10 hrs. | Quantity: 4-6 servings |

3 tablespoons flour

1½ pounds beef stew, cut into 1-inch cubes

1 beef bouillon cube

½ cup water

2 medium onions, chopped

1 medium green pepper, chopped

2 large garlic cloves, crushed*

1 tablespoon paprika

1 teaspoon caraway seed

½ teaspoon salt

¼ teaspoon pepper

1. Place flour in large zip-top plastic bag; add beef and shake to coat. Drop in crockpot.
2. Dissolve bouillon cube in water; add to beef with onions, green peppers, garlic, paprika, caraway seeds, salt and pepper.
3. Cover and cook for 5-6 hours on high or 10-12 hours on low.

HINT: Serve with egg noodles and salad.

*Use chopped or minced ready to use garlic in the jar for convenience.

LANSING CHILI

This is actually a version of Cincinnati Chili, but I thought Lansing needed some press, too. The ingredient list is long but very easy. This makes a huge quantity which freezes wonderfully and can be pulled from the freezer and ready in minutes!!!

| Prep time: 20 min. | Cook time: 1 hr. 30 min. | Quantity: 8-10 servings |

2 pounds ground beef

7 cups water

1 can (32-ounce) crushed tomatoes

1 can (12-ounce) tomato paste

2 large onions, chopped

2 bay leaves

4 tablespoons chili powder

2 tablespoons cocoa powder—yes cocoa powder

2 cloves garlic, crushed*

2 tablespoons cider vinegar

2 teaspoons ground cinnamon

2 teaspoons ground cumin

2 teaspoons salt

½ teaspoon ground cloves

1. In a large pot, place beef and water and stir to break up meat.
2. Simmer over medium heat for 15 minutes or until meat loses its red color; skim off foam with spoon. Stir in the rest of the ingredients.
3. Simmer over low heat for 1 hour and 30 minutes; stir occasionally; cover pan partially so sauce does not get too thick.
4. Suggestions on how to serve chili are below. Enjoy!

How to Serve

Serve chili on top of cooked spaghetti. Serve with kidney beans, chopped onion, finely grated cheddar cheese and oyster crackers to sprinkle on top.

HINT: This recipe makes enough for 2 pounds of spaghetti.

Use chopped or minced ready-to-use garlic in the jar for convenience.

ZUCCHINI LASAGNA

You will be surprised how easy this is. The entire family will love it. There will be a lot of juice with this dish so make sure you include a nice loaf of crusty bread with the meal to soak up the yummy juices.

| Prep time: 12 min. | Bake time: 325°/40 min. | Quantity: 4 servings |

½ pound ground beef or turkey

1 can (8-oz.) tomato sauce

2 teaspoons Italian seasoning

1 teaspoon salt

½ teaspoon garlic powder

4 cups zucchini, sliced in ¼-inch discs

1 cup small curd cottage cheese

1 cup grated mozzarella cheese

1. Preheat oven to 325 degrees.
2. Coat an 8-inch square baking dish with non-stick cooking spray.
3. In a medium skillet, brown meat; stir in tomato sauce, Italian seasoning, salt and garlic powder.
4. Arrange half of the zucchini slices in the bottom of baking dish. Spoon half of the meat sauce, half of the cottage cheese and half of the mozzarella cheese over the zucchini.
5. Repeat the layering, ending with the mozzarella cheese.
6. Bake uncovered for 40 minutes.
7. Serve.

HINT: This dish can be made at the beginning of the day and refrigerated until ready to put in the oven. Increase the baking time 10-15 minutes.

VEGGIE CHILI

This recipe is for those who need a break from red meat chili. It is loaded with great things and the meat is not missed at all.

Prep time: 15 min.   Cook time: 20-30 min.   Quantity: 6 servings

¼ cup vegetable oil

2 large onions, chopped

3 cans (14-ounce each) diced tomatoes

2 cans (7-ounce each) mushroom pieces

2 cups broccoli, cut up

2 cups zucchini, sliced

1 whole green pepper, cored, seeded and chopped

¼ cup chili powder

1 teaspoon garlic powder

¼ teaspoon black pepper

2 cans (15½-ounce each) kidney beans, drained

¼ cup water

2 teaspoons flour

1. In a large saucepan, warm oil over medium-high heat. Add onions and sauté until softened, about 8 minutes; reduce heat to medium.

2. Add tomatoes, mushrooms, broccoli, zucchini, green pepper, chili powder, garlic powder and black pepper. Cover and simmer for 15-30 minutes; stir occasionally.

3. In a small bowl, combine water and flour with whisk. Stir into chili and add beans. Cook until thickened, about 5 minutes or until beans are warmed through; stir frequently.

4. Serve.

HINT: This chili can be served alone or over rice, pasta or couscous. The quantity of veggies is approximate—do not try to measure perfectly. Try serving with chopped green onion, sour cream or cheddar cheese. This chili freezes well.

MEXICAN LASAGNA

Quick, easy and great tasting!

Prep time: 15 min.   Bake time: 400°/15 min.   Quantity: 4-6 servings

2 tablespoons vegetable oil

1¼ pounds ground turkey

1 medium onion, chopped

1 green pepper, chopped

1 can (4-ounce) green chilies, diced

1 package (1.25-ounce) taco seasoning mix

1 bottle (10-ounce) taco sauce

1 package (10 count) flour tortilla (divided in half)

2 cups grated cheese, your choice

1. Preheat oven to 400 degrees.
2. Coat a 9x13-inch baking pan with non-stick cooking spray.
3. In a large skillet, warm oil over medium heat. Add turkey and sauté until no longer pink, about 6-8 minutes. Stir in onion, pepper, chilies and seasoning mix. Reduce heat to low and cook for 3-4 minutes; stir occasionally.
4. In the baking pan, spread ¼ cup taco sauce over bottom; cover with 5 tortillas. Spread tortillas with half of the turkey mixture, half of remaining taco sauce and 1 cup of cheese. Repeat with remaining ingredients (tortilla, turkey, sauce and then cheese).
5. Bake for 15-20 minutes or until heated through and cheese melts.

HINT: If casserole is made the morning of serving, place in refrigerator until ready to bake and increase baking time by 15 minutes or until heated through.

CHEESE ENCHILADAS

A good friend gave me this recipe a long time ago. I have used it often when serving a large crowd. The recipe is fun, easy and 'loose'. My friend, Chris Catt, tested this. Her husband liked it so much he ate half the dish before dinner! I hope you like it just as much.

| Prep time: 10 min. | Bake time: 350°/25 min. | Quantity: 8-10 servings |

Sauce

2 cans (10¾-ounce each) cream of chicken soup

1 cup sour cream

1-2 cans (4-ounce each) chopped green chilies *(mild)*

Filling

2½ cups cheddar cheese, grated

1 bunch green onions, chopped *Sauteed white onion)*

1½ cups *cooked* chicken, cubed

1 c. olives (sliced)

1 package (18-count) corn tortillas

1. Preheat oven to 350 degrees.

2. Coat a 9x13-inch baking dish with non-stick cooking spray.

3. In a medium bowl, combine sauce ingredients; whisk until combined.

4. In a separate medium bowl, combine filling ingredients; toss with a fork.

5. Spread ½ cup sauce in bottom of baking dish, cover with ⅓ of the tortillas (breaking in half if needed) and ⅓ of filling mixture. Continue layering the sauce, tortillas and filling, making 3-4 layers ending with sauce.

6. Bake for 25 minutes or until bubbly.

7. Serve.

HINT: Using canned chicken saves a lot of time with this recipe and works just as well. This dish freezes well before baking and also freezes or refrigerates well after baking. Increase bake time by 20-30 minutes for frozen/unbaked dish or 10-20 minutes for refrigerated dish.

TUNA SWISS PIE

This dish came from an old friend. She always cooked easy, carefree dishes that took minimal amounts of time so she could visit with friends. I have since made this recipe for wedding and baby showers as well as potlucks for Boy Scouts.

Prep time: 10 min.	Bake time: 375°/50 min.	Quantity: 6 servings

1 – 9-inch pastry shell, baked

2 cans (6-ounce each) tuna, drained and flaked

1 cup Swiss cheese, grated

1 bunch green onions, chopped

3 large eggs

1 cup mayonnaise

½ cup milk

1. Preheat oven to 375 degrees.
2. In a large bowl, combine tuna, Swiss cheese and onion; toss together. Place in pastry shell.
3. In same large bowl, beat eggs, mayonnaise and milk together; pour slowly on top of tuna mixture.
4. Bake 50 minutes or until knife inserted in center comes out clean.

HINT: You can make and bake ahead and freeze the pie. Reheat in oven or microwave when ready to eat.

AWESOME SANDWICH

The title describes it, nothing more needs to be said. I have made this so many times I can do it in my sleep. It is always on the top of the list for a weekend lunch.

| Prep time: 30 min. | Bake time: 350°/35 min. | Quantity: 6 servings |

1 pound frozen bread dough, thawed

1 tablespoon olive oil

1 large garlic clove, crushed*

¼ pound salami, thinly sliced

¼ pound provolone cheese, sliced

1 jar (7-ounce) roasted red peppers, drained, sliced in 4-inch strips

2 green onions, chopped

1. Preheat oven to 350 degrees.
2. Stretch bread dough out into 12-inch square and place on parchment lined baking sheet; spread olive oil and garlic over dough.
3. Spread salami and cheese slices down middle third of dough with slight overlap, top with roasted red peppers, and green onions.
4. Slice bread dough with kitchen shears or sharp knife by making eight 3-inch long cuts along both sides of filling. Bring dough strips up across filling at slight angle, alternating sides to create braided effect; seal ends with a pinch.
5. Let sit for 20-30 minutes in a warm quiet area in kitchen. Bake for 35 minutes or until golden brown. Cool for 5 minutes and serve warm or cold.

HINT: I have also used half ham, half salami for variety. Travels well from the refrigerator to the car or from the microwave to the table.

*Use chopped or minced ready to use garlic in the jar for convenience.

BREAKFAST PIZZA

Great for breakfast, lunch or dinner. Also great to take 'on the go' since it slices easily and stays in one piece in the car.

Prep time: 20 min.	Bake time: 375°/20 min.	Quantity: 8 servings

1 pound frozen bread dough, thawed

1 tablespoon sesame seeds

¼ cup ham, diced

¼ teaspoon salt

⅛ teaspoon pepper

4 large eggs

¼ cup milk

3 green onions, sliced

1 cup cheddar cheese, grated

1. Preheat oven to 375 degrees.
2. Line a 12-14-inch round pizza pan or 9x13-inch baking pan generously overlapping sides of pan with foil.
3. On a lightly floured surface, roll bread dough to approximately fit into pan; use hands to stretch dough if necessary. Pinch edges to form a low standing rim.
4. In a medium bowl, beat eggs until blended. Brush a little of the beaten egg on edge of dough and sprinkle sesame seeds onto edge of dough.
5. Bake crust for 5 minutes.
6. Meanwhile in the same bowl, combine milk, ham, green onions, salt and pepper; beat together until blended.
7. Remove crust from oven. Make a collar, slightly higher than the crust, with the foil that lines the pan to keep the egg from escaping. Pour egg mixture into partially baked pizza crust; return to oven, immediately. Bake 20 minutes or until egg is set.
8. Remove from oven and top pizza with cheese. Let pizza sit for 2 minutes or until cheese is melted.
9. Cut into 8 wedges and serve.

HINT: You can add any number of items on the pizza at step '6', pepperoni, onion, mushrooms, or even cooked breakfast sausage!

BAKED FRENCH TOAST SOUFFLÉ

If you are like me and can never remember to make these overnight casseroles the night before—this recipe is very forgiving. You can make this in the morning and let it rest at least 45 minutes before baking and it still turns out crispy on the edges and yummy inside!

Prep time: 20 min./overnight	Bake time: 350°/35 min.	Quantity: 10 servings

1 pound (16-ounce) loaf French bread, not sliced

8 large eggs, beaten slightly

3 cups milk

2 tablespoons sugar

1 teaspoon vanilla

¼ teaspoon salt

½ teaspoon cinnamon

¼ teaspoon nutmeg

1 cup brown sugar

1 cup pecans, chopped (optional)

½ cup butter, softened

2 tablespoons light corn syrup

½ teaspoon each cinnamon and nutmeg

1. Preheat oven to 350 degrees.
2. Coat a 10x15-inch baking dish with non-stick cooking spray.
3. Cut bread into 20 equal slices. Arrange bread slices in one layer, overlapping slices if necessary.
4. In a medium bowl, combine eggs, milk, sugar, vanilla, salt, cinnamon, and nutmeg. Pour mixture over bread slices; cover and chill overnight (see note below recipe title).
5. In small bowl, combine brown sugar, pecans, butter, corn syrup, ½ teaspoon cinnamon and ½ teaspoon nutmeg with fork until paste forms—about 45 seconds. Crumble/spread sugar mixture over bread.
6. Bake in preheated oven for 35-40 minutes or until browned.
7. Serve.

NOTE: With this recipe you don't need syrup!!!!

ANDREA'S CINNAMON PANCAKES

Andrea is awesome in the kitchen and on the soccer field—these pancakes of hers are the best!

Prep time: 8 min.	Cook time: 4 min.	Quantity: 12 servings

2 cups dry pancake mix (the just-add-water kind)

½ cup water

1 teaspoon vanilla

½ teaspoon cinnamon

1. In a large bowl, mix all ingredients, do not over mix the batter.
2. Test your griddle with a drop of water—it should sizzle.
3. Pour out the pancake batter on the griddle and cook until bubbles in pancake begin to pop.
4. Slide your spatula under the pancake and flip; cook until golden brown.
5. Serve hot with melted butter and warm syrup.

NOTE: "I've been making these pancakes since I was 8½ years old. They taste great the night before a game too!" — Andrea Zaworski.

*When cooking with your children **always** remind them to be very careful around the electric or gas stove. I suggest constant supervision while working with children in the kitchen.*

DARN—OUT OF PANCAKE SYRUP!

This is a handy recipe and will save you many times when it's 10 A.M. on a Sunday morning, the cakes are on the griddle, and you realize you are out of syrup. You will thank me again and again.

| Prep time: 5 min. | Microwave time: 1 min. | Quantity: approx. 1¼ cups |

¼ cup brown sugar

¼ teaspoon salt

¼ teaspoon maple extract

¾ cup light corn syrup

¼ cup water

1. Combine all ingredients in a microwaveable bowl. Cook on high until sugar melts and all ingredients are combined, about 1 minute.
2. Serve warm or store in refrigerator for up to 1 month.

HINT: Maple extract is a great flavoring to have on hand for this recipe as well as an addition to a nut muffin or pound cake recipe for a new flavor.

5-MINUTE PIZZA SAUCE

If you are the type of family that likes to make your own pizza but likes the convenience of the pre-made crusts, this sauce will work perfectly for you. It tastes like professional pizza sauce from the pizzeria!

| Prep time: 5 min. | Cook time: none | Quantity: enough for 2 – 12-inch pizzas |

1 can (28-ounce) crushed tomatoes in puree

1 tablespoon dried oregano

2 large cloves garlic, crushed*

1 tablespoon dried basil

1 teaspoon onion flakes

½ teaspoon salt

¼ teaspoon black pepper

¼ teaspoon garlic powder

¼ teaspoon sugar

1. Combine all the above ingredients and let sit for 5 minutes before using.

HINT: This can be frozen for up to 2 months.

*Use chopped or minced ready to use garlic in the jar for convenience.

GREAT COUNTRY MARINADE

Marinades are a great way for making a quick meal special. This marinade is excellent with chicken, turkey or pork!

| Prep time: 5 min. | Cook time: none | Quantity: enough for 2-3 pounds of meat |

⅓ cup cider vinegar

2 tablespoons Dijon mustard

2 tablespoons vegetable oil

3 teaspoons dried basil

½ teaspoon salt

1 teaspoon grated lemon peel

1 large clove garlic, crushed*

1. In a small bowl, combine all the above ingredients; whisk. Place in freezer type zip-top storage bag.
2. Add your choice of meat and marinate for 2-24 hours.
3. Remove meat from marinade, discard any marinade and grill, broil or fry.

Use chopped or minced ready to use garlic in the jar for convenience.

LEMON MARINADE

Light and refreshing for chicken or pork.

| Prep time: 2 min. | Marinate time: 4-8 hrs. | Quantity: enough for 2-3 pounds of meat |

1 can (6-ounce) frozen concentrated lemonade, thawed

¾ cup soy sauce

3 green onions, chopped (optional)

1. Combine above ingredients; toss in freezer type zip-top storage bag with chicken or pork.
2. Marinate up to 1 day; bake or grill.

HINT: Here is a quick marinade idea: After combining marinade ingredients and chicken in freezer type zip-top storage bag, place directly in freezer for up to 2 months; thaw in refrigerator the day you are ready to cook. The meat will be tender and perfectly seasoned every time.

RED AND WHITE MEAT MARINADE

Great Mediterranean flavor!

| Prep time: 5 min. | Marinate time: 5-6 hrs. | Quantity: enough for 3-4 pounds meat |

½ cup olive oil

¼ cup balsamic vinegar

3–4 large cloves garlic, crushed*

¼ cup fresh parsley, chopped

¼–½ teaspoon black pepper

Salt

1. In a small bowl, whisk all ingredients together. Place marinade and meat in a freezer type zip-top storage bag; marinate for 5-6 hours, turn occasionally if possible.
2. Grill, broil, roast or pan-fry until desired doneness.
3. Salt meat when done cooking to preserve the juices and tenderness.

HINT: No need to marinate in the refrigerator when making in advance. After combining marinade ingredients and meat in freezer type zip-top storage bag, place directly in freezer for up to 2 months; thaw in refrigerator the day you are ready to cook.

*Use chopped or minced ready to use garlic in the jar for convenience.

THROW-INS

This chapter contains many great side dishes to compliment any main dish you may be preparing. Some of these can also be served as a main dish! My side dishes are simple and uncomplicated, using frozen or fresh vegetables to create the most convenient and nutritious dish. Make sure you flip through all the pages of this chapter—there are many new and creative ways to make side dishes your family will love.

Throw-Ins

GREENZ AND CHEESE

Have the kids grate the cheese while you chop the broccoli. They will be more likely to eat their vegetables when they have something to do with the preparation!

Prep time: 5 min.   Cook time: 10 min.   Quantity: 4 servings

1 bunch broccoli, cut up

⅓ cup evaporated milk

1½ cups cheddar cheese, grated

1. Pour water in bottom of large skillet to 1-inch depth; bring to boil over medium-high heat. Add broccoli and cover tightly with lid.
2. Steam for 5-7 minutes or until broccoli is crisp/tender.
3. While the broccoli is steaming, combine the milk and cheese in small microwaveable bowl. Microwave for 1-2 minutes or until cheese melts and sauce is smooth; stir occasionally.
4. Remove the broccoli from heat and drain water off; place broccoli in serving dish.
5. Pour sauce over broccoli and serve.

GREEN BEAN SAUTÉ

This is perfect with chicken on the grill.

| Prep time: 5 min. | Cook time: 8 min. | Quantity: 4 servings |

1 bag (16-ounce) green beans, frozen

3 tablespoons olive oil

1 small onion, chopped

1 large garlic clove, crushed*

¼ cup Parmesan cheese, grated

3 tablespoons red wine vinegar

1. Steam the beans as package directs and keep warm in shallow serving dish; drain if necessary.
2. In a medium skillet, warm oil over medium heat. Add onions and garlic; sauté for 8 minutes.
3. Pour over beans in serving dish, sprinkle with cheese and vinegar; toss well.
4. Serve immediately.

Use chopped or minced ready to use garlic in the jar for convenience.

SEASONED GREEN BEANS

My friend, Cindy, loves this dish. It is very flavorful and a nice twist on the basic green bean.

| Prep time: 2 min. | Microwave time: approx. 8 min. | Quantity: 6 servings |

1 pound frozen green beans

½–1 teaspoon onion flakes

½–1 teaspoon dried minced garlic

¼ teaspoon salt

⅛ teaspoon black pepper

1. Place frozen beans in microwaveable bowl; sprinkle with remaining ingredients; toss to coat.
2. Place plastic wrap over bowl and cook in microwave on high for 4 minutes; toss beans and microwave for 4 more minutes.
3. Serve.

ZESTY CARROTS

This recipe is a winner. Carrots are so easy to prepare and are loaded with vitamins and nutrients. "The horseradish adds an interesting touch." —*Eddie Jones*

Prep time: 5 min.   Bake time: 375°/15 min.   Quantity: 4 servings

Throw-Ins

6 large carrots, peeled and sliced into ¼-inch discs

2 tablespoons horseradish

2 tablespoons onion, grated

½ cup mayonnaise

1 teaspoon salt

¼ teaspoon pepper

¼ cup water

¼ cup breadcrumbs

1 tablespoon butter, melted

1. Preheat oven to 375 degrees.
2. Coat a 6x10-inch baking dish with non-stick cooking spray.
3. Cook carrots in water until tender; drain; place in prepared baking dish.
4. In a small bowl, combine horseradish, onion, mayonnaise, salt, pepper and ¼ cup water; mix well.
5. Pour horseradish mixture over carrots; sprinkle with breadcrumbs and butter. Bake 15 minutes.
6. Serve.

TARRAGON CARROTS

One of my husband's favorites.

| Prep time: 5 min. | Microwave time: approx. 8 min. | Quantity: 4 servings |

1 pound carrots, peeled (about 3-4 large carrots)

1 tablespoon dried tarragon

2 tablespoons butter, room temperature

¼ teaspoon salt

1. Slice carrots crosswise to ½-inch thickness.
2. Place carrots in shallow microwaveable casserole dish with 1 tablespoon of water; cover tightly with plastic wrap. Microwave on high until barely fork tender, about 4-6 minutes.
3. Add butter, salt and tarragon to hot carrots; stir well to combine. Cover tightly with plastic wrap and microwave for 1 minute.
4. Serve immediately.

HINT: Try fresh slender green beans! The microwave times may vary.

CARROT TOSS

A great way to dress up carrots. Surprise the family with a simple vegetable that tastes great!

Prep time: 5 min.   Cook time: 10 min.   Quantity: 6 servings

8 tablespoons butter or margarine

1 large onion, sliced thinly

6 carrots, peeled and sliced thinly

1 tablespoon sugar

2 teaspoons dried tarragon

Salt and pepper to taste

1. In a large skillet, warm butter over medium heat. Add onion and cook for 3 minutes; stir occasionally.
2. Increase heat to medium-high and add carrots; stir until carrots are crisp-tender about 4-5 minutes.
3. Sprinkle with sugar and tarragon and cook for 2 more minutes.
4. Season with salt and pepper and serve.

CHEDDAR ONION PUDDING PIE

The creamy richness makes this pie a winner with kids and adults. My neighbor made this a long time ago when I lived in Detroit. I must have eaten half the pie one evening while visiting, which convinced the neighbor to give me the recipe on the spot! I have used different cheeses, added diced jalapeno or a can of green chilies on different occasions. My kids love this dish—even my daughter who cringes at the sight of onions.

| Prep time: 10 min. | Bake time: 400°/30 min. | Quantity: 6-8 servings |

2 tablespoons butter or margarine

1 medium onion, chopped

1½ cups milk

1 large egg, beaten

1½ cups Bisquick®

1 cup cheddar cheese, grated (divided in half)

2 tablespoons butter or margarine, melted

Salt and pepper to taste

1. Preheat oven to 400 degrees.
2. Coat a 9-inch pie pan with non-stick cooking spray.
3. In a medium skillet, warm butter over medium-high heat. Sauté onion in butter for 8 minutes or until golden brown; set aside.
4. In a large bowl, combine milk and egg; blend in Bisquick®, ½ cup of cheese, and sautéed onion mixture.
5. Pour into pie pan and sprinkle with remaining ½ cup of cheese.
6. Drizzle with melted butter and sprinkle with salt and pepper. Bake for 30 minutes.
7. Cool slightly, cut and serve.

HINT: This dish freezes well! Try Monterey Jack or Swiss cheese in place of the cheddar for a change.

CHEESY ZUCCHINI BAKE

Great recipe when the garden is overflowing with zucchini!

| Prep time: 10 min. | Bake time: 350°/35 min. | Quantity: 4-6 servings |

Throw-Ins

2 tablespoons vegetable oil

1 large onion, chopped

4 cups zucchini, thinly sliced (about 3-4 med. zucchini)

1 tablespoon dried oregano

½ teaspoon garlic powder (optional)

¾ teaspoon salt

¼ teaspoon pepper

1 cup mozzarella or provolone cheese, grated

½ cup ricotta cheese (not low-fat)

2 large eggs, beaten

1. Preheat oven to 350 degrees.
2. Coat an 8x12-inch or 9x9-inch baking dish with non-stick cooking spray.
3. In a large skillet, warm oil over medium-high heat. Add onion, zucchini, oregano, garlic powder, salt and pepper; sauté for 5 minutes.
4. Remove from heat and drain any liquid that may have collected in bottom of pan. Add mozzarella, ricotta, and eggs; toss gently coating zucchini well.
5. Fill prepared baking dish with vegetable mixture.
6. Bake uncovered for 35 minutes or until top is browned.
7. Serve.

HINT: Can be made in advance and frozen before baking. Increase the bake time by approximately 15 minutes or until heated through and top is browned.

ZUCCHINI AU GRATIN

Nice and fresh. This dish has a slightly tart taste from the fresh zucchini. If you want a sweeter taste use dried sweet basil or a pinch or two of sugar when adding the salt and pepper.

| Prep time: 5 min. | Cook time: 15 min. | Quantity: 6 servings |

2 tablespoons olive oil

4 cups zucchini, thinly sliced (approx. 3-4 medium zucchini)

1 large onion, thinly sliced

2 teaspoons dried oregano

Salt and pepper to taste

3 tablespoons Parmesan cheese

1. In a large skillet, warm oil over medium-high heat.
2. Add zucchini, onion, oregano, salt and pepper to skillet; stir to coat.
3. Reduce heat to medium; cover and cook for 2 minutes; remove lid and sauté for 10 minutes.
4. Sprinkle with cheese, remove from heat and serve.

HINT: Another great recipe when the garden is overflowing with zucchini!

SUPER-QUICK SEASONED VEGGIES

*A **real** easy way to serve vegetables to the family with great flavor and very little effort.*

| Prep time: 2 min. | Cook time: 10 min. | Quantity: 4 servings |

2 cups fresh or frozen vegetables—broccoli, green beans, carrot or zucchini

2 cups water

1-2 chicken bouillon cubes

1. Bring water and bouillon to a boil until bouillon is dissolved.
2. Add vegetables and bring to a simmer; cook until vegetables are crisp-tender.
3. Drain and serve hot, room temperature or cold.

CAMP VEGGIES

My husband's family camped for years and this is one of the unique ways they made their vegetables over the campfire. We have also taken on the tradition of summer camping and making 'camp veggies'. I have taken the liberty of adding a few different seasonings for a new taste. We have also used this method over our grill at home, which always brings back the camp memories quickly. You don't have to have the exact ingredients listed. Experiment!

Prep time: 5 min.   Grill time: approx. 15-20 min.   Quantity: 4-6 servings

2 large sheets of **_heavy duty foil_**

1 large onion, chopped

2 small zucchini, chopped

2 green pepper, chopped

2 small yellow squash, chopped

A handful of mushrooms, halved

½ head broccoli, chopped

2 large garlic cloves, crushed*

1 teaspoon dried basil

½ teaspoon salt

¼ teaspoon pepper

2-4 tablespoons margarine (the easy squeeze kind works great for this job!)

1. Lay out the 2 sheets of foil on counter for two packets.
2. Evenly distribute all the vegetables over the two sheets of foil; sprinkle with basil, salt and pepper.
3. Place 1-2 tablespoons of margarine on top of each mound of vegetables. Seal up tightly by double folding all the edges of the foil. Can be made up to 5 hours in advance.
4. Place over fire or grill turning every 3-4 minutes. Grill time is between 15-20 minutes, depending on heat source.
5. Remove from grill and serve right in pocket.

HINT: Olive oil can be used in place of margarine, for a slightly more sophisticated taste.

*Use chopped or minced ready to use garlic in the jar for convenience.

APPLE BEAN BAKE

Interesting rich flavor!

Prep time: 10 min.	Bake time: 375°/1 hr.	Quantity: 8-10 servings

1 jar (48-ounce) great northern beans, drained

4 tablespoons butter or margarine

3 cups Granny Smith apples, peeled, cored and chopped

1 red onion, roughly chopped

³⁄₄ cup brown sugar

½ cup ketchup

1 teaspoon cinnamon

¼ teaspoon ground cloves

1½ teaspoons salt

1. Preheat oven to 375 degrees.
2. Coat casserole dish with non-stick cooking spray.
3. In a large skillet, melt butter over medium heat; add apples and onions. Cook for 10 minutes; stir occasionally.
4. Add brown sugar, ketchup, cinnamon, cloves and salt; stir well.
5. Place beans in prepared casserole dish. Pour apple mixture over the beans; mix well. Bake for 1 hour. (Cover beans during baking process if drying out too much.)

TEXAS BOY BEANS

A great recipe I picked up while in Texas. The kids love the taste and I love the ease of it. This dish actually tastes like you slaved all day over the stove.

Prep time: 20 min.   Bake time: 350°/30 min.   Quantity: 8 servings

6 slices bacon

1 large onion, chopped

½ cup ketchup

¼ cup brown sugar

1 tablespoon vinegar (cider or white)

½ teaspoon salt

1 tablespoon prepared mustard

1 can (16-ounce) pork and beans

1 can (15½-ounce) kidney beans, drained

1 can (15½-ounce) lima beans, drained

1. Preheat oven to 350 degrees.
2. Coat a 9x13-inch glass ovenproof baking dish with non-stick cooking spray.
3. Cook bacon until crisp in large skillet. Remove bacon and crumble in large mixing bowl. Add onions to skillet containing bacon grease and cook for 8 minutes.
4. Remove cooked onions from bacon grease (discarding grease), and place in bowl with the crumbled bacon; add remaining ingredients; mix well.
5. Pour into prepared baking dish. Bake for 30 minutes.

HINT: This recipe can be made and refrigerated up to 2 days before baking. You may need to increase the baking time by 10 minutes.

KICK'N BEAN BAKE

The lime juice and salsa add a great southwest flair to this dish!

Prep time: 2 min.   Bake time: 375°/15 min.   Quantity: 8 servings

Throw-Ins

1 can (16-ounce) baked beans

1½ cups chunky salsa, any flavor

1 tablespoon lime juice

1 cup crushed tortilla chips

1 cup Monterey Jack cheese, grated

1. Preheat oven to 375 degrees.
2. Coat a 9x13-inch baking pan with non-stick cooking spray.
3. In a large bowl, combine beans, salsa and lime juice. Place bean mixture in prepared baking pan; sprinkle with chips.
4. Bake for 12 minutes; sprinkle with cheese.
5. Bake for 2 more minutes and serve.

HINT: Can be made up to 3 days in advance and re-warmed in oven or microwave.

MONSTER POTATO PANCAKE

The rosemary makes this a perfect side dish for roasted chicken. Quick, easy and delicious—the kids love the presentation, too!

| Prep time: 10 min. | Cook time: 15 min. | Quantity: 6-8 servings |

4-5 medium russet potatoes, peeled and shredded

4 tablespoons butter

½ teaspoon rosemary, crumbled

½ teaspoon salt

¼ teaspoon pepper

1. In a large skillet, warm butter over medium heat.
2. Pat the pile of shredded potatoes with paper towels to dry and place in large bowl; toss with rosemary, salt and pepper.
3. Spread evenly in skillet; pat down firmly with spatula.
4. Cook until crisp on bottom, about 7-8 minutes.
5. Invert onto serving plate and slide back into pan. Cook another 7-8 minutes or until crisp.
6. Transfer to plate and serve.

HINT: You can use different spices in place of rosemary, such as oregano, tarragon, basil or none at all. Most adults like the rosemary and most kids like it plain. Also, a food processor really speeds up the shredding process.

QUICK POTATO BAKE

"Very easy to prepare!" —*Lynn and Larry Ezzo*

Prep time: 5 min.	Microwave time: 5 min.	Quantity: 4 servings	Bake time: 10 min. (optional)

4 medium russet potatoes, sliced ¼-inch thick

2 tablespoons vegetable oil

¼ teaspoon salt

¼ teaspoon garlic powder

⅛ teaspoon black pepper

1. In a microwaveable/ovenproof casserole dish, toss potatoes, vegetable oil, salt, garlic powder and pepper.
2. Cover tightly with plastic wrap.
3. Microwave on high for 5 minutes.

Crispy Option

Microwave just the potatoes tossed with oil. Remove from microwave and toss with remainder of ingredients and bake at 450 degrees for 10 minutes or until desired crispness.

> *HINT: Potatoes can be peeled and wrapped in damp paper towels and stored in zip-top storage bag in refrigerator up to 3 days.*

JOEY'S PILLOW POTATOES

My son loves to make this recipe. It tastes great and is one less thing I have to worry about for the dinner hour when he offers to make this recipe.

Prep time: 15 min.	Microwave time: 10 min.	Broil time: 2 min.	Quantity: 6 servings

3 large russet baking potatoes

3 tablespoons butter or margarine

½ cup milk

½ teaspoon salt

¼ teaspoon pepper

2 cups cheddar cheese, grated

3 tablespoons Parmesan cheese, grated (optional)

1. Scrub potatoes and pierce with a fork several times to prevent exploding in microwave.
2. Place in microwave and cook for 10 minutes or until fork tender.
3. Slice in half lengthwise. While still hot, scoop out potato with a spoon and place in a medium mixing bowl (not necessary to get all the potato out of shell); place on cookie sheet.
4. Mash the potato with butter, milk, salt and pepper; mix in half the cheddar cheese; spoon the potato mixture back into the shells.
5. Top with remaining cheddar cheese and sprinkle with Parmesan cheese.
6. Place under the broiler for 2 minutes or until cheese just melts.
7. Serve!

CREAMY POTATO BAKE

This dish is a hit with kids and adults. I have made this in advance and frozen it for many Thanksgiving dinners. It is rich, yummy and everything a person should expect from a potato casserole!

Prep time: 10 min.	Bake time: 350°/30 min.	Quantity: 4-6 servings

3 cups hot mashed potatoes (instant potatoes work great in this dish!)

1 cup sour cream

¼ cup milk

¼ teaspoon garlic powder

1 cup cheddar cheese, grated, divided

⅔ cup canned French fried onions

1. Preheat oven to 350 degrees.
2. Coat a 2-quart casserole dish with non-stick cooking spray.
3. In a medium bowl combine potatoes, sour cream, milk, garlic powder and ½ cup cheddar cheese; mix well.
4. Place half of potato mixture in casserole dish; sprinkle with fried onions. Place remaining potatoes on top.
5. Bake for 30 minutes; remove from oven, sprinkle with remaining cheddar cheese; rest for 5 minutes.
6. Serve.

HINT: This dish freezes well.

TACO POPPERS

These potatoes have a great taco flavor! The kids may even ask for them as a snack!

| Prep time: 10 min. | Microwave time: 6 min. | Bake time: 450°/8 min. | Quantity: 4 servings |

4-5 medium russet potatoes

¼ cup vegetable oil

1 package (1¼-ounce) taco seasoning mix

3 tablespoons cornmeal

1. Preheat oven to 450 degrees.
2. Pierce potatoes with a fork and place in microwave. Microwave for 6 minutes or until barely tender.
3. Cut in large cubes and place in large mixing bowl; toss with vegetable oil.
4. Combine taco seasoning and cornmeal in a large zip-top storage bag.
5. Place potatoes in taco seasoning bag; shake to coat.
6. Place on un-greased baking sheet. Bake 8 minutes or until golden brown.

POTATOES MONACO

Easy and has a light taste—great flavor! Perfect potato dish to accompany grilled chicken in the summer.

| Prep time: 15 min. | Bake time: 350°/10 min. | Quantity: 4 servings |

1¾ cups milk

4 potatoes, peeled and cut into 1½-inch chunks

½ teaspoon salt

¼ teaspoon pepper

1 tablespoon butter sprinkles (found in the seasoning aisle)

¼ cup feta cheese, crumbled

1 tablespoon breadcrumbs

Salt and pepper

1. Preheat oven to 350 degrees.
2. Coat a 2-quart baking dish with non-stick cooking spray.
3. In a large saucepan, combine milk and potatoes. Simmer over medium heat until potatoes are tender, about 10 minutes. Stir occasionally to avoid scorching pan, adding more milk if necessary.
4. Remove saucepan from heat. Using slotted spoon, transfer potatoes to large baking dish; reserve milk.
5. Whisk salt, pepper and butter sprinkles into reserved milk and pour over potatoes.
6. Sprinkle potatoes with cheese and breadcrumbs. Bake for 10 minutes.
7. Serve immediately or refrigerate up to 2 days in advance. Re-warm in oven or microwave.

Throw-Ins

MICRO-POTATO

The green peppers add a distinct flavor to this dish.

Prep time: 5 min.   Microwave time: 15 min.   Quantity: 6 servings

¼ cup butter

1½ teaspoons salt

¼ teaspoon pepper

4 medium potatoes, peeled and sliced 1/8-inch thick

½ large green pepper, chopped

1 medium onion, chopped

1. In a medium microwaveable casserole dish, melt butter; stir in salt and pepper.
2. Add remaining ingredients to casserole dish; toss well until coated with butter.
3. Cover and microwave on high; stir every 3 minutes or until potatoes are fork tender, about 10-12 minutes.
4. Let stand 10 minutes.
5. Serve!

POTATO PIE

I have served this for breakfast with fresh fruit as well as a side dish for dinner. It is a very flexible dish that the kids will eat as an after school snack too!

Prep time: 8 min.   Bake time: 350°/40 min.   Quantity: 6 servings

6 large eggs *3 eggs*

½ cup milk *¼ c. milk*

4 3 cups frozen hash brown potatoes, any style

1 bunch green onions, chopped *(optional)*

½ teaspoon salt

2-3 dashes hot sauce (such as Tabasco®) *McCormick Mex seas.*

1½ cups cheddar cheese, grated

⅓ cup bacon bits

2 T butter

Large cooktop fry pan w/ 2T butter

1. Preheat oven to 350 degrees.

2. Coat a 9-inch pie pan with non-stick cooking spray.

3.*a* In a large bowl, beat eggs and milk together; stir in remaining ingredients. *except cheese*

3 b Brown potatoes on 1 side fry pan w/ butter

4. Pour mixture into pie pan. Bake for 40-45 minutes or until center is set. *12*

Add cheese/egg to top of potatoes   Saute covered for 10 mins

5. Remove from oven; rest for 5 minutes.

6. Serve. *warm*   *heat, sprinkle bacon bits on top*

LESS FAT CHEESEY POTATOES

For those of you who are looking for a great potato dish that has all the richness of the 'old time potato casserole' with a lot less fat—here it is! It is undeniably the best low-fat potato dish that I have put together out of my many trials—creamy and rich and loaded with a lot of flavor.

> Prep time: 15 min.   Bake time: 400°/50 min.   Quantity: 6-8 servings

1 cup cottage cheese (2% fat)

4 ounces low-fat cream cheese, softened

1 tablespoon dried basil

4 large potatoes, peeled and sliced ¼-inch thick

½ cup milk, *skim*

2 tablespoons all-purpose flour

Salt and pepper to taste

⅓ cup Parmesan cheese, grated

1. Preheat oven to 400 degrees.
2. Coat 9x13-inch baking pan with non-stick cooking spray.
3. In blender, combine cottage and low-fat cream cheese. Blend until all lumps are gone* (scraping the blender bowl a few times will help the process). Add basil; blend until combined.
4. In a small bowl, whisk milk and flour until smooth; set aside.
5. Arrange one-third of potatoes in bottom of pan. Spread potatoes with half creamy cheese sauce; sprinkle with salt and pepper.
6. Repeat once again with one-third of potatoes and remainder of sauce, salt and pepper.
7. Add final layer of potato; sprinkle with Parmesan cheese; pour milk over top.
8. Bake uncovered for 50 minutes or until potatoes are tender and golden brown.
9. Serve.

* Add 1-2 tablespoons of skim milk to thin slightly, only if needed.

SWEET POTATO CLASSIC

This dish is a classic plate on the Thanksgiving Day table. Instead of using fresh sweet potatoes I opted to use canned potatoes to make the dish a bit easier.

Prep time: 10 min.   Bake time: 350°/20 min.   Quantity: 4-6 servings

Throw-Ins

2 cans (29-ounce each) yams or sweet potatoes, drained and cut into large chunks

¼ cup butter or margarine, melted

¼ cup orange juice

½ teaspoon cinnamon

¼ teaspoon salt

⅛ teaspoon ground cloves

15 large marshmallows

1. Preheat oven to 350 degrees.
2. Coat 2-quart casserole dish with non-stick cooking spray.
3. In a large bowl, combine potatoes, butter, orange juice, cinnamon, salt and cloves; mix well.
4. Spoon potato mixture into dish. Bake for 20 minutes.
5. Sprinkle with marshmallows and let sit for 5 minutes. Serve!

HINT: This dish can be made in the microwave by using a microwaveable dish. Microwave potato mixture on high for 4 minutes, stir, and microwave for 4 more minutes. Remove from microwave and top with marshmallows; allow dish to sit for 5 minutes before serving.

HOP AND POP FRIED RICE

This recipe is great when you need a starch for a deli bought chicken. The dish is very mild and perfect for young kids. My sons Cub Scout Pack 264 was having an end of the year picnic and I brought a huge bowl of this—it disappeared before any of the adults went through the food line!

Prep time: 5 min.   Cook time: 25 min.   Quantity: 6-8 servings

6 cups *cooked* instant rice, warm or room temperature

3 tablespoons vegetable oil

1 medium onion, diced

1 stalk celery, diced

2 large eggs, beaten

1 cup frozen peas and carrots

1 can (14-ounce) bean sprouts, drained

1 bunch green onions, chopped

2-3 tablespoons soy sauce

1. Cook instant rice as the package directs; set aside.
2. When ready to prepare dish, heat oil in large fry pan over medium-high heat; add onions and cook for 5 minutes. Add celery and cook for 5 more minutes.
3. Add the eggs and stir until set, about 3-4 minutes; break up cooked egg.
4. Add frozen peas and carrots; cover with lid and turn down heat to medium-low; cook for 5 minutes.
5. Add the rice and stir until rice is heated through, about 5 minutes.
6. Transfer to a large serving bowl; add sprouts and green onions; sprinkle with soy sauce. Stir gently and serve.

HINT: A couple more tablespoons of soy sauce can be added just before serving.

MAGICAL VEGGIE RICE DISH

Nice creamy texture with the crunch of vegetables!

Prep time: 12 min.   Cook time: 15 min.   Quantity: 6 servings

2 cups chopped broccoli

2 carrots, peeled and sliced

1 red pepper, chopped

1 medium onion, chopped

2 tablespoons bacon bits

3 cups instant rice, **_cooked_** and kept warm

4 tablespoons butter or margarine

1 teaspoon dried oregano

⅓ cup Parmesan cheese, grated

Salt and pepper to taste

1. **_Steam_** the broccoli, carrots, red pepper and onion together until broccoli is tender, about 4-5 minutes.
2. Add bacon bits to the steamer and steam 1 additional minute.
3. Place the steamed vegetables in a large serving bowl; toss with warm rice, margarine, oregano and cheese.
4. Salt and pepper to taste.
5. Serve immediately.

HINT: This can be doubled and served as a main dish.

QUICK RICE PUDDING

Rice pudding was a special dish in our house when growing up. My mom would slave at the oven for over an hour stirring this 'stuff' in a baking dish. It seemed to take all day. I have modified my mom's recipe to make it easier and quicker for my lifestyle. All you need is cooked rice left over from the night before or instant rice works just as well.

Prep time: 5 min.   Cook time: 15 min.   Quantity: 6 servings

½ cup sugar

⅓ cup all-purpose flour

¼ teaspoon salt

2½ cups milk

2 cups cooked rice

2 large eggs

½ cup golden raisins (optional)

½ teaspoon cinnamon

¼ teaspoon nutmeg

1 tablespoon vanilla extract

1. In a medium saucepan, combine sugar, flour and salt; whisk in milk until smooth; add rice.
2. Cook over medium heat, stirring constantly, until mixture comes to a boil, about 10 minutes. Boil for 2 more minutes and remove from heat.
3. In a small bowl, beat eggs. Slowly add 1 ladle of hot pudding into eggs while stirring. Slowly pour beaten egg mixture back into pudding mixture; mix quickly and thoroughly.
4. Add raisins, cinnamon, nutmeg and vanilla.
5. Return to heat and cook for 3 more minutes; stir constantly. Pour into 1 large shallow serving bowl.
6. Serve hot, warm or cold.

HINT: This is a great dish to serve with pork or lamb. It can also be served cold with warm milk and a generous sprinkle of cinnamon.

GREAT GARLIC BREAD

*This is the best homemade garlic bread you will ever taste! Real garlic bread with **real** taste!*

| Prep time: 5 min. | Bake time: 450°/5 min. | Quantity: 8 servings |

½ cup **butter**, room temperature

½ cup romano cheese, grated

¼ cup **fresh** Italian parsley, chopped

¼ teaspoon pepper

2-3 large garlic cloves, crushed*

1 large loaf Italian bread, halved lengthwise

1. Preheat oven to 450 degrees.
2. In a medium bowl combine butter, cheese, parsley, pepper and garlic; blend well.
3. Spread butter mixture over sliced sides of bread; place on baking sheet.
4. Bake until bubbly and golden brown, about 5 minutes.
5. Serve immediately.

*HINT: Butter and spice mix **OR** the whole loaf can be prepared 1 day ahead and refrigerated at this point or frozen for up to 1 month. Bring to room temperature before continuing.*

*Use chopped or minced ready to use garlic in the jar for convenience.

SEASONED BISCUITS

Wonderful combination of herbs to compliment a chicken dish with gravy.

Prep time: 3 min.   Bake time: 375°/14 min.   Quantity: 8 biscuits

1 container (10-ounce) Pillsbury Grand® biscuits

2 tablespoons margarine, melted

Select any combination of seasonings:

 ½ teaspoon rosemary crushed

 ½-1 teaspoon garlic powder

 1 tablespoon grated Parmesan cheese

 ¼ teaspoon Italian seasonings

 ¼ teaspoon parsley

 ¼ teaspoon dried minced onion

1. Preheat oven to 375 degrees.
2. Place biscuits in single layer in a baking pan.
3. Combine seasonings in bowl with melted margarine; mix well.
4. Spread seasoned butter over biscuits.
5. Bake for 14-16 minutes or until golden brown (watching carefully not to burn bottoms of biscuits).
6. Serve hot.

OVERTIME

Who doesn't like dessert? A lot of easy and great tasting
treats—from cakes to pies to cookies to fruit dips to ice
cream—you can always find a sweet for a treat in this
chapter. Enjoy every last bite—I know I did!

Overtime

PUMPKIN PECAN BUNDT CAKE

This bundt cake is moist, delicious, so darn easy and freezes well. I make this recipe, cut the bundt cake into quarters and freeze them individually so I can take out smaller quantities— depending on how many children or adults I am serving.

| Prep time: 12 min. | Bake time: 325°/60 min. | Quantity: 12 servings |

3 cups all-purpose flour

2 tablespoons pumpkin pie spice

2 teaspoons baking soda

1 teaspoon salt

2 sticks butter or margarine, softened

2 cups brown sugar

4 large eggs

1 can (15-ounce) pumpkin

¾ cup pecans or walnuts, chopped

1. Preheat oven to 325 degrees.
2. Coat a bundt pan with non-stick cooking spray.
3. In a medium bowl, combine flour, pie spice, baking soda, and salt with whisk; set aside.
4. In a large bowl, beat together the butter and brown sugar until light and fluffy, about 2 minutes. Add eggs and pumpkin to butter mixture; combine well.
5. Add flour mixture and mix just until combined.
6. Sprinkle nuts in bottom of bundt pan; spoon batter gently into pan.
7. Bake for 60 minutes or until tester comes out clean. Cool for **5 minutes**, then invert onto cake rack to cool completely.

HINT: To make drizzle for the cake, take ½ cup canned vanilla or coconut pecan frosting and warm in microwave. Drizzle over cake and cool.

Overtime

CARAMEL APPLE CAKE

I have made this for years and the kids just love it. The hardest part of the recipe is peeling, coring and slicing the apples. The rest is easy and can be served as a snack or dessert with French vanilla ice cream or sweetened whipped cream.

| Prep time: 10 min. | Total bake time: 350°/40 min. | Quantity: 18 slices |

1 box (18.25-ounce) spice cake mix

1 cup quick oats

1 cup walnuts or pecans, chopped

1 large egg

½ cup margarine, melted

2 Granny Smith apples, peeled, cored and thinly sliced

3 tablespoons all-purpose flour

1 cup caramel ice cream topping

1. Preheat oven to 350 degrees.
2. Spray 9x13-inch pan with non-stick cooking spray.
3. Combine cake mix, oats, and nuts in large bowl; add egg and margarine with fork or pastry blender until crumbly.
4. Press 3 cups of crumb mixture into bottom of prepared pan. Bake for 8 minutes.
5. Remove from oven and place apples evenly over top of crust.
6. Whisk flour into caramel topping and pour over top of apples; sprinkle with remaining crumbs. Bake for 30-35 more minutes.

HINT: Great when served warm or at room temperature.

APPLE SUGAR CAKE

Sweet and simple to prepare—this cake is perfect for the family who likes their cake and wants to eat it too—especially when no one can be around all day to make a cake from scratch.

Prep time: 10 min.   Bake time: 375°/30 min.   Quantity: 12 servings

1 large egg, beaten

¼ cup milk

¼ cup margarine, melted, cooled slightly

1 teaspoon vanilla

1 box (18.25-ounce) spice cake mix

1 large Granny Smith apple, cored and sliced
(no need to peel)

Streusel Topping

1 tablespoon brown sugar

1 tablespoon white sugar

1 tablespoon margarine softened

½ teaspoon cinnamon

1. Preheat oven to 375 degrees.
2. Coat a 9x9-inch pan with non-stick cooking spray.
3. In a small bowl, combine egg, milk, margarine and vanilla; mix well.
4. Place cake mix in a large bowl. Add the wet ingredients to the cake mix and make a smooth batter by mixing for 1 minute.
5. Spread batter into prepared pan and place apples evenly over top of batter.
6. Combine the streusel toppings in same small bowl with fingers and sprinkle over top of apples.
7. Bake for 30-35 minutes.
8. Cool before serving.

HINT: Can use butter cake mix if preferred. Makes a very nice breakfast cake, too!

Overtime

STRUDEL CREAM CHEESECAKE

Incredibly creamy and smooth. Anybody with a sweet tooth will love this dessert.

> Prep time: 20 min.   Bake time: 350°/25 min.   Quantity: 12 servings

2 containers (8-ounce each) crescent rolls

2 packages (8-ounce each) cream cheese, room temperature

1 cup sugar

1 teaspoon vanilla

¼ cup butter, softened

¼ - ½ cup apricot preserves (optional)

Topping

½ cup all-purpose flour, ¼ cup sugar, ¼ cup butter (room temperature)

½ cup slivered almonds

1. Preheat oven to 350 degrees.
2. Remove crescent roll dough from 1 container and cover entire bottom of 9x13-inch cake pan, using fingers to seal all seams.
3. In a medium mixing bowl, combine cream cheese, sugar, vanilla and butter; mix well. Spread mixture over crescent rolls. Drop apricot preserves by teaspoon over top of cream cheese mixture.
4. Open remaining crescent roll container and place the dough gently over top of cream cheese mixture, gently sealing seams, as best you can, with fingers.
5. Combine topping ingredients with fork and spread over top of crescent dough; sprinkle with almonds. Bake for 25 minutes.
6. Cool in pan 5 minutes and then enjoy!

CLASSIC MINI CHEESECAKES

This recipe is a classic and is so easy. Ages from 1-99 love this treat and it's perfect for the mom who wants to make those special comfort foods with limited time.

| Prep time: 10 min. | Bake time: 350°/20 min. | Quantity: 30 muffin cups |

4 packages (8-ounce each) cream cheese, softened

1¼ cups sugar

2 tablespoons vanilla

4 large eggs

30 vanilla wafer cookies,

1 can (21-ounce) pie filling, cherry or blueberry

1. Preheat oven to 350 degrees.
2. In a mixer, cream the cream cheese; add the sugar, vanilla and eggs. Cream mixture until no lumps appear.
3. Line regular sized muffin tins with paper cup liners and place one wafer cookie in each cup.
4. Pour cream cheese mixture into each cup to ¾ full.
5. Bake for 20 minutes.
6. Cool and top with pie filling or serve plain.

HINT: For a patriotic look that doesn't take much time, top each cheesecake with a teaspoon each of cherry and blueberry pie filling and whipped topping. Assemble completely with the toppings and freeze in a single layer up to 2 months. Thaw and store in refrigerator.

KID TEST RESULTS: *Sarah—12 on a scale of 1-10*
Hannah—Nice, creamy, light, very extremely good. Excellent.
Zach—Really good, delicious 'x2' terrific!

Overtime

FOOLS STRAWBERRY CHEESECAKE

Don't let the title fool you! You actually stack this dessert in a glass and you don't have to bake it! A long time ago a neighbor taught me the secret of combining strawberries and brown sugar with sour cream to create a luscious cheesecake flavor. I took the idea a bit farther and made this dessert.

Prep time: 15 min.	Bake time: none	Quantity: makes approx. 4 servings

1 cup sour cream

¼ cup brown sugar

1 cup vanilla yogurt

3 cups strawberries, rinsed, hulled and sliced

1. In a medium bowl, combine sour cream and brown sugar; mix well.
2. In four parfait glasses or dessert cups, layer strawberries, ¼ cup sour cream mixture and then ¼ cup yogurt.
3. Repeat layer one more time.
4. Store up to 1 day in refrigerator.
5. Sprinkle with brown sugar right before serving.

HINT: Blueberries or sweet cherries work well with this dessert, too. Serving the dessert frozen is also a great twist.

SUMMER CAKES

A very refreshing, healthy, easy and fast recipe. It is perfect as a dessert with chicken salad and greens!

Prep time: 5 min.   Bake time: none   Quantity: 6-8 servings

6-8 large short cakes, baked or store bought

3 kiwi, sliced

1 large banana, sliced

1 pint sliced strawberries, blueberries or raspberries

1 can (8-ounce) pineapple chunks, drained

Whipped topping

1. Make a quick batch of short cakes or buy at grocery store.
2. Any time the day of serving combine the kiwi, bananas, strawberries, and pineapple chunks in a bowl and refrigerate.
3. After dinner is served, split the shortcakes and dress with the fruit.
4. Top with whipped topping and serve.

INCREDIBLE DOUBLE CHOCOLATE COOKIE

This recipe is done by hand and in this case is actually quicker than using a mixer. Just make sure the butter is at room temperature. This recipe is just the ticket to make before the kids get home from school—you'll even be able to sneak one cookie before they arrive home.

| Prep time: 10 min. | Bake time: 350°/10 min. | Quantity: approx. 36 cookies |

1½ cups chocolate chips

½ cup brown sugar

¼ cup sugar

¼ cup butter, ***room temperature***

2 large eggs

1 teaspoon vanilla

1¼ cups all-purpose flour

1 teaspoon baking powder

1 package (8-ounce) semisweet chocolate baking squares, coarsely chopped

2 cups nuts, chopped (optional)

1. Preheat oven to 350 degrees.
2. In a large microwaveable bowl, melt 1½ cups chocolate chips in microwave. It takes about 1-2 minutes on high. Remember to stir every 30 seconds so the chocolate does not scorch.
3. Stir the brown sugar and white sugar, butter, eggs and vanilla into the melted chocolate immediately; mix until butter is melted. Add flour and baking powder; stir until combined.
4. Stir in chopped baking squares and nuts. Drop by heaping tablespoon-full onto un-greased cookie sheets.
5. Bake 10 minutes for soft middles or 12 minutes for crispy cookies.
6. Remove from oven; cool for one minute.
7. Remove from cookie sheet and cool completely on rack.

GINGER COOKIES

These cookies are a snap and a hit with the neighborhood kids. They keep forever and are great to take along on long rides to those out of town games.

Prep time: 10 min.	Bake time: 350°/10 min.	Quantity: 3½ dozen

⅔ cup vegetable oil

1 cup sugar

1 large egg, slightly beaten

¼ cup molasses

2 cups all-purpose flour

2 teaspoons baking soda

½ teaspoon salt

1 teaspoon cinnamon

2 teaspoons ground ginger

1. Preheat oven to 350 degrees.
2. Combine all the ingredients in heavy-duty mixer; mix well.
3. Roll dough into balls about the size of a walnut.
4. Place balls on un-greased cookie sheet and press down slightly; sprinkle sugar over tops of each cookie.
5. Bake for 10 minutes; cool on wire racks.

HINT: Store in airtight container on counter for up to 1 week. These cookies freeze beautifully for up to 2 months. Excellent with vanilla ice cream.

Overtime

APPLESAUCE COOKIES

Soft and comforting—I have made these cookies since my children were babies. They are always heartwarming and a great snack I can give the kids after school. I sometimes make a double batch and freeze a portion of them to pop into lunch boxes or to have a plateful ready for the unexpected guest.

| Prep time: 5 min. | Bake time: 375°/10 min. | Quantity: 2 dozen |

1 cup brown sugar

¾ cup margarine, softened

1 large egg

½ cup applesauce

2¼ cups all-purpose flour

½ teaspoon baking soda

½ teaspoon salt

1 teaspoon cinnamon

¼ teaspoon cloves

1. Preheat oven to 375 degrees.
2. In a large bowl, cream brown sugar, margarine and egg; stir in applesauce.
3. Add flour, baking soda, salt, cinnamon and cloves; mix well.
4. Drop by heaping teaspoon onto greased cookie sheet 1½–2-inches apart.
5. Bake for 10-12 minutes. Remove from cookie sheet and cool on racks.

HINT: You can add ½ cup of walnuts and/or raisins to the batter when adding the cinnamon and cloves. You can also drizzle icing over the cooled cookies for a fancy look.

COOKIE CUPS

Easy and fast! The kids love them so you may want to make 2 batches—one for home and the other for the game!

| Prep time: 10 min. | Bake time: 375°/13 min. | Quantity: 24 mini cups |

1 package (18-ounce) refrigerated chocolate chip cookie dough

24 chocolate kisses, mini peanut butter cups or 2 cups of M&Ms®

1. Preheat oven to 375 degrees.
2. Spray mini muffin tins lightly with non-stick cooking spray. Scoop 1 level tablespoon of dough into each mini muffin tin. Bake for 12 minutes.
3. Remove from oven and place a chocolate kiss, mini peanut butter cup or 1 tablespoon of M&Ms® in each cup; press down gently.
4. Bake for 1 minute more, just for candy to melt.
5. Cool slightly before removing from pan.

SWEET TREAT COOKIE SANDWICHES

Surprise your kids with this easy sweet-treat. I sometimes make these cookie sandwiches with ice cream, but the filling recipe below makes for an easy item to transport in a lunch box, bring to a game or a picnic. You can also make them in advance and freeze ahead of time. They are perfect to bring to an end of the season game. Perfect for birthday party treats at school, too!

| Prep time: 10 min. | Cook time: none | Quantity: 6 sandwiches |

12 chocolate chip cookies; store bought, about 2½-inch diameter

2 tablespoons butter, softened

1 cup powdered sugar, sifted (divided)

2 teaspoons milk

½-1 teaspoon extract or flavoring; vanilla, peppermint, almond, lemon, or orange

1 tablespoon multicolored sprinkles

1. In a small bowl, beat butter and **_half_** the powdered sugar until smooth. Add milk, remaining powdered sugar, flavoring and sprinkles; beat until well combined.
2. Spread frosting on bottom side of chocolate cookie and top with another cookie making a sandwich. There is enough frosting for 6 sandwiches.
3. Store in refrigerator; wrap in plastic when firm.

HINT: You can make the frosting in advance and store in refrigerator until ready to frost the cookies. The whole cookie sandwich can be made in advance, wrapped individually and frozen. A great 'grab and go' snack!

WHITE JERSEY PIZZA

Great stuff for the kids to make themselves or serve for a sleepover party.

Prep time: 10 min.   Microwave time: approx. 2 min.   Quantity: 16 servings

8-10 ounces white chocolate

2 cups crisp rice cereal

1 cup miniature marshmallows (divided)

½ cup peanuts ~~dried~~ *cranberries* + ½ cup walnuts/pecans

16 chocolate kisses

NO 8 maraschino cherries cut in half *(optional berries)*

1. Coat a 10-12-inch round pizza pan with butter.
2. In a large microwaveable bowl, melt white chocolate in microwave.
3. Add cereal, ½ cup marshmallows and ~~peanuts~~ *cranb* to melted white chocolate; mix well. Spread in pizza pan making an approximate 10-inch circle.
4. Melt chocolate kisses in microwave. Drizzle over pizza and decorate with maraschino cherries and marshmallows.
5. Cool in refrigerator for 15 minutes and serve.

HINT: In place of peanuts, I have used almond brickle. Also, try adding peanut butter chips for a different flavor.

BUTTERSCOTCH CRUNCH

This is one of the easiest recipes in this book. I have made this for many bake sales and potluck dinners—people always ask for the recipe.

Prep time: 5 min.	Microwave time: approx. 1-2 min.	Quantity: 25 squares

1 cup butterscotch chips

½ cup peanut butter (creamy or crunchy)

1 cup crispy rice cereal

1 cup dry roasted peanuts

1. In a large microwaveable bowl, combine chips and peanut butter. Microwave on high for 30 seconds; stir well.
2. Continue on high for 30 seconds at a time until melted and combined. Add rice cereal and nuts; mix well.
3. Pour into 8x8-inch baking pan and refrigerate until firm.
4. Cut into 25 squares and serve.

HINT: You can use blanched peanuts instead of dry roasted peanuts. You can also use cocoa rice cereal in place of regular rice cereal. Experimenting with this recipe is what makes it so much fun. Believe it or not, this freezes beautifully.

*"I love this recipe!! I'm not patient enough to be a good baker, but these are **so easy** and **delicious**." —Linda Dufelmeier.*

CHEWY CHOCOLATE FRUIT CLUSTERS

Great for holiday gifts. It doesn't take a lot of time and no baking is required. The best part is that not a lot of pans get dirty—a definite plus!

Prep time: 10 min.	Microwave time: 2 min.	Quantity: 24 clusters

1 cup chocolate chips

½ cup walnuts, coarsely chopped

⅓ cup raisins

½ cup whole oats

1. In a large microwaveable bowl, melt chocolate in microwave on high for 45 seconds to 1 minute; stir halfway through the cook time. Remove from microwave and stir the chocolate until smooth.
2. Add the nuts, raisins and oats to the chocolate; stir until well combined.
3. Drop chocolate mixture by heaping teaspoon on waxed lined cookie sheets; cool in refrigerator.
4. Store in a cool, dry location. Keeps up to 2 weeks.

HINT: Cashews or pecans can be substituted for the walnuts, and dried chopped apricots are a great substitute for the raisins.

Overtime

SIMPLE S'MORE DESSERT

When my son turned 8, we celebrated his birthday by hosting a camp cookout. He chose to have a S'more cake. All the boys loved it! We actually made it over the campfire. This is close to the recipe, a bit more refined, but still sticky, yummy and messy all in the same bite—just the way it should be!

Prep time: 10 min.	Bake time: 350°/25 min.	Quantity: 12-16 servings

½ cup butter or margarine, cut into 8 pieces

1½ cups graham cracker crumbs

1 can (14-ounce) sweetened condensed milk

1 cup chocolate chips

1 cup miniature marshmallows

1. Preheat oven to 350 degrees.
2. Place butter in a 9x13-inch baking pan and place in oven for 2-3 minutes to melt butter.
3. Remove from oven and sprinkle crumbs evenly over butter.
4. Pour condensed milk evenly over top of crumbs; sprinkle with chocolate chips; press gently to firm up the crust. Bake for 25 minutes.
5. Remove from oven and sprinkle with marshmallows; bake for 2 more minutes.
6. Cool completely before serving (if you can wait that long)!

QUICK COOKIE SQUARES

This pan of cookies will disappear before you turn around. You may want to make two pans just in case!

Prep time: 10 min.   Bake time: 350°/30 min.   Quantity: 25 squares

1¼ cups powdered sugar

1½ cups peanut butter

1½ teaspoons vanilla

1 package (18-ounce) refrigerated chocolate chip cookie dough

1. Preheat oven to 350 degrees.
2. In a mixing bowl, combine sugar, peanut butter and vanilla; mix well.
3. Using floured fingers, remove cookie dough from wrapper and press <u>one half</u> of dough into bottom of 9-inch square pan. (Add optional toppings at this point—see HINT.)
4. Press peanut butter mixture over top of dough.
5. Crumble rest of cookie dough over peanut butter as evenly as possible.
6. Bake for 30-35 minutes or until golden brown.
7. Cool completely in pan on wire rack, slice and serve.

HINT: Try different kinds of refrigerated dough flavors for more variety. Cookie squares would also be good with ½ cup of various toppings such as mini M&Ms®, butterscotch morsels, or peanut butter chips.

Overtime

COOKIE PIZZA

Kids of all ages love this kind of pizza.

Prep time: 10 min.   Bake time: 350°/16 min.   Quantity: 12-14 servings

1 package (20-ounce) refrigerated sugar cookie dough

½ cup dry roasted peanuts, chopped

1 cup miniature marshmallows

1 cup chocolate chips

⅓ cup caramel ice cream topping

1. Preheat oven to 350 degrees.
2. Slice cookie dough as directed on package. With cookie dough slices make a 12-inch circle on large baking sheet, (overlapping cookie dough slices slightly). Fill in circle with remaining sliced cookie dough; seal firmly with fingertips.
3. Bake for 16-18 minutes; remove from oven.
4. Sprinkle cookie with peanuts, marshmallows and chocolate chips; drizzle with caramel topping.
5. Bake for 2-4 minutes longer or until marshmallows are golden brown.
6. Cool for 10 minutes or longer. Slice.

FRUIT PIZZA

Great and refreshing for after the game when the kids are at your house drinking juice and eating, eating and eating some more!

Prep time: 10 min.   Bake time: 350°/14 min.   Quantity: 8 servings

1 package (20-ounce) refrigerated sugar cookie dough

1 package (8-ounce) cream cheese, softened

⅓ cup sugar

1 teaspoon vanilla

1 can (20-ounce) pineapple rings, drained

1 large banana, sliced

1 kiwi, sliced

¼ cup strawberries, raspberries or blueberries

¼ cup apricot jam

1. Preheat oven to 350 degrees.
2. Press cookie dough into 14-inch pizza pan and bake for 14-16 minutes; cool.
3. While cookie is cooling, beat cream cheese, sugar and vanilla until blended; spread over cooled cookie.
4. Arrange the fruit on top of the cream cheese.
5. Place apricot jam in small microwaveable bowl. Microwave for 15-20 seconds (until jam melts). Brush apricot jam over the fruit.
6. Serve immediately or refrigerate until ready to serve.

DEBBY'S CARAMEL APPLE CHEESECAKE PIE

My sister-in-law loves to bake but doesn't always have the time because of her work schedule and busy family life. She made this recipe for Thanksgiving a couple of years ago and it was the first thing that disappeared from the dessert table ... even before the pumpkin pie!

Prep time: 15 min.	Bake time: 350°/35 min.	Quantity: 8 servings

1 can (21-ounce) apple pie filling (divided)

1 – 9-inch graham cracker crust

2 packages (8-ounce each) cream cheese, room temperature

½ cup sugar

½ teaspoon vanilla

2 large eggs, slightly beaten

⅓ cup caramel ice cream topping

12 pecan or walnut halves (optional)

2 tablespoons chopped nuts (optional)

1. Preheat oven to 350 degrees.
2. Reserve ¾ cup of apple pie filling. Spoon rest of filling into bottom of crust; set aside.
3. In a medium bowl, beat cream cheese, sugar and vanilla; add eggs and beat until smooth. Pour over apples in piecrust.
4. Bake for 35 minutes; cool.
5. Mix reserved apple filling and caramel topping together in small saucepan; bring to a boil. Cook for 1 minute; stir gently and constantly.
6. Gently spread over top of cooled pie; spread evenly; decorate with pecan halves and sprinkle with chopped nuts.
7. Refrigerate until ready to serve.

PICKET FENCE APPLE PIE

A simple pie to make and the homemade taste is beyond compare.

| Prep time: 10 min. | Bake time: 375°/50-60 min. | Quantity: 6 servings |

1 - 9-inch unbaked pie shell

6 cups Granny Smith apples, peeled, cored and sliced

1 tablespoon lemon juice

$\frac{3}{4}$ cup sugar, brown or white

3 tablespoons all-purpose flour

$\frac{1}{2}$ teaspoon cinnamon

$\frac{1}{3}$ cup raisins, dried cherries, or chopped dates

Crumb Topping

1 cup oats

$\frac{1}{2}$ teaspoon cinnamon

$\frac{1}{3}$ cup brown sugar

$\frac{1}{3}$ cup margarine, melted

1. Preheat oven to 375 degrees.
2. In a large bowl, toss apples with lemon juice.
3. In a small bowl, combine sugar, flour and cinnamon. Add to apples with your choice of dried fruit; toss. Pour into pie shell.
4. In same small bowl, combine 'crumb topping' ingredients together with fingers; sprinkle on top of apples. Press down slightly to hold together.
5. Bake for 50-60 minutes or until topping is brown.
6. Serve warm or cold!

GO USA PIE

This pie has a very patriotic appearance.

Prep time: 10 min.	Freeze time: 1 hr. minimum	Quantity: 8 servings

1 8 or 9-inch ready-made graham cracker crust

1 quart ice cream, (your favorite flavor), softened

1 cup whipped topping

1 cup strawberries, halved

1 cup blueberries

1 cup miniature marshmallows

1. Fill crust with ice cream and then gently cover with whipped topping.
2. Arrange strawberries, blueberries and marshmallows on top.
3. Place pie on cookie sheet and place in the freezer, on a level surface, immediately.
4. Freeze at minimum for 1 hour and up to 2 months.
5. Remove from freezer 10-20 minutes before serving.

HINT: For a nice change try peaches and raspberries in place of strawberries and blueberries.

PEANUT BUTTER PIE

*An **outstanding** dessert! Always have this recipe handy because kids love it and so do adults. I have had it forever and **every time** I take this pie somewhere someone inevitably asks for the recipe... so here it is folks!!!*

Prep time: 8 min.   Freeze time: 4 hrs.   Quantity: 6-8 servings

4 ounces cream cheese, softened

⅓ cup creamy peanut butter

⅓ cup **whole milk**

½ cup powdered sugar

1 container (8-ounce) non-dairy whipped topping, thawed

1 – 9-inch graham cracker crust

1. In a medium bowl, beat cream cheese until smooth, about 1 minute.
2. Add peanut butter and beat for 30 seconds more.
3. Add milk and powdered sugar, alternately beating after each addition; scrape bowl occasionally.
4. Blend in whipped topping.
5. Pour into piecrust and freeze 4 hours.
6. It can be served chilled or frozen. Store in refrigerator.

FRESH PEACH PIE

Lauren Zaworski invited a few soccer families over one hot summer evening for grilling and swimming. It was a very impromptu event so everyone brought a dish to pass that was easy, simple and quick. One family, originally from Georgia, brought this pie. It was eaten before the main course was served!

Prep time: 8 min.	Chill time: 1 hr.	Quantity: 6-8 servings

¼ cup butter, softened

1 cup powdered sugar, sifted

1 tablespoon brandy

1 – 9-inch pie shell, baked and cooled as directed

6 large ripe peaches, peeled and sliced

3 tablespoons *fresh lemon juice*

¼ cup sugar

3 tablespoons powdered sugar for garnish

1. In a medium bowl, beat butter until creamy, about 1 minute.
2. Add powdered sugar and brandy to butter; mix well. Spread in bottom of pie shell; chill for 20 minutes.
3. In a medium bowl, combine peaches, lemon juice and ¼ cup sugar; toss gently.
4. Arrange on top of creamed mixture in pie shell; chill for 1 hour.
5. Serve.

HINT: Peaches will come loose when slicing pie—just rearrange on plates when serving. Great with side of vanilla ice cream.

CHOCOLATE CHIP COOKIE PIE

This dessert is rich and a perfect comfort food. My friend, Willie Busch, loved serving this dessert topped with whipped cream. Making two pies and freezing one is a good idea. It is very easy to put together and it looks great when served as a wedge instead of the typical round cookie on a plate.

Prep time: 10 min.	Bake time: 350°/50-60 min.	Quantity: 8 servings

1 – 9-inch deep-dish pastry shell, _uncooked_

2 large eggs

½ cup all-purpose flour

1 cup brown sugar

1 cup butter or margarine, melted and cooled

1 cup chocolate chips

1 cup walnuts, chopped (optional)

1. Preheat oven to 350 degrees.
2. Have pastry shell ready. Beat eggs until frothy, about 3 minutes.
3. Add flour and sugar and beat well, about 1 minute. Add butter slowly; blend well.
4. Stir in chocolate chips and walnuts; pour into pie shell.
5. Bake for 1 hour. Serve warm or room temperature.

HINT: Whipped cream, ice cream or chocolate sauces are all favorite additions to this dessert.

FALL APPLE CRISP

Apples are at their best in the fall anywhere in the U.S. Take advantage of this fabulous fruit and make this dish—in the microwave to save time. Serve with French vanilla ice cream!

Prep time: 12 min.	Microwave time: 15 min.	Quantity: 8 servings

6 Granny Smith apples

1½ cups graham cracker crumbs

¾ cup brown sugar

½ cup oats

½ cup all-purpose flour

1 teaspoon cinnamon

½ teaspoon nutmeg

½ cup butter or margarine, melted

1. Peel, core and slice apples (this is the time consuming part) and place in 2-quart microwaveable baking dish.
2. In a medium bowl, combine graham cracker crumbs, brown sugar, oats, flour, cinnamon, nutmeg and butter; mix well.
3. Sprinkle over apples and microwave on high for 6 minutes. Rearrange dish and microwave for 7 more minutes or until apples are tender.
4. Serve warm.

APPLE POPPER

This is an exceptional way to use canned biscuit dough without revealing the shortcut. Kids love the simple flavors and it is an excellent dessert after a family meal.

Prep time: 12 min.   Bake time: 350°/25-30 min.   Quantity: 8 servings

1 container (16-ounce) biscuit dough (reduced fat works great!)

¾ cup brown sugar

2 teaspoons cinnamon

6 tablespoons butter or margarine, melted

2 large Granny Smith apples, peeled, cored and sliced ¼-inch thick wedges

½ cup chopped walnuts (optional)

1. Preheat oven to 350 degrees.
2. Coat an 8x12-inch or 9x13-inch baking pan with non-stick cooking spray.
3. In a shallow bowl, combine brown sugar and cinnamon. Place melted butter in a separate shallow bowl.
4. Remove biscuits from container and coat both sides of biscuit in melted butter and then in brown sugar mixture (reserving left over butter and sugar).
5. Place biscuits in baking pan—squeezing them in if necessary to make 1 layer.
6. Place apple slices between, around and on top of biscuits.
7. Sprinkle with nuts if desired and then with reserved brown sugar and butter.
8. Bake for 25-30 minutes or until golden brown.

HINT: Can be prepared earlier in the day and refrigerated until ready to bake. Allow 3-5 minutes additional baking time if refrigerated.

BAKED APPLES

Simple and perfect for fresh fall apples. Kids and adults love this dessert.

Prep time: 10 min.	Bake time: 375°/40 min.	Quantity: 4 servings

4 large tart apples (such as Granny Smith)

¼ cup brown sugar

1 teaspoon cinnamon

4 teaspoons margarine

1. Preheat oven to 375 degrees.
2. Wash and remove core to ½-inch of bottom of apple and place on baking sheet.
3. In a small bowl, combine sugar and cinnamon; fill the cored apples.
4. Place 1 teaspoon margarine on top of each filled core.
5. Bake uncovered for 40-45 minutes or until tender.
6. Remove from oven and baste with pan juices (if any) several times before serving.

HINT: If you want to make a big hit with the family—serve with French vanilla ice cream and caramel sauce. Watch them lick their fingers!

EASY FRESH FRUIT TARTS

Make the wonton cups in advance and just fill them when ready to serve. Great healthy dessert.

| Prep time: 20 min. | Bake time: 375°/6 min. | Quantity: 12 mini tarts |

12 wonton skins*

2 tablespoons apricot jam

1 cup lowfat yogurt (your choice of flavor)

1¼ cups fresh fruit, cut up

1. Preheat oven to 375 degrees.
2. Coat 12 mini-muffin cups lightly with non-stick cooking spray.
3. Press each wonton skin into each muffin cup letting edges of wonton skin hang over edge of muffin tin.
4. Spray wonton skins with non-stick cooking spray. Bake for 6-8 minutes or until slightly brown. Remove wonton wraps from muffin tin carefully; cool on rack.
5. Warm apricot jam in microwave until jam melts; approximately 20 seconds.
6. Spread melted jam in bottom of cooled wonton cups; fill with yogurt and fresh fruit.
7. Serve immediately.

HINT: The wonton cups can be made up to 1 week in advance; store in an airtight container.

*Normally found in produce section of your grocery store.

Overtime

EASY LEMON ICE CREAM

I make this dessert for Christmas day and serve it after the 'big meal'. Everyone finds it very refreshing and a nice compliment to the Christmas cookie tray. No one will know how quick and easy it is! You can also serve this dish on a hot summer day with store bought pirouettes and everyone will think that you've turned into a gourmet cook—just don't tell them your secret!

Prep time: 10 min.	Freeze time: 4 hrs.	Quantity: 8-10 servings

2 cups whipping cream

1 cup sugar

Grated peel of 1 lemon

⅓ cup **_fresh_** lemon juice

1. In a large bowl, combine cream and sugar. **_Stir until sugar is dissolved_** (this may take up to 5 minutes).
2. Add lemon peel and juice; stir for 10 seconds. Mixture will begin to thicken.
3. Pour into shallow pan. Freeze for at least 4 hours.
4. Serve.

SANDWICH COOKIE ICE CREAM

I have had this recipe forever and do not remember where it came from. This is really one of my favorite ice cream dessert recipes of all time. It covers all the bases for me: cookies, whipped cream and easy!

| Prep time: 10 min. | Freeze time: 6 hrs. | Quantity: 8 servings |

3 large egg yolks

1 can (14-ounce) sweetened condensed milk

2 tablespoons water

4 teaspoons vanilla extract

1 cup coarsely crushed chocolate sandwich cookies

2 cups (1 pint) whipping cream (make sure you *do not* use whipped topping)

1. Whip the whipping cream until soft peaks form; set aside.
2. Crush the cookies and set aside*.
3. Line a 9x5-inch loaf pan with aluminum foil.
4. In large bowl beat egg yolks for 1 minute. Stir in sweetened condensed milk, water and vanilla; fold in cookies and whipping cream. Pour into lined loaf pan.
5. Freeze for 6 hours or until firm.
6. When ready to serve, remove block of ice cream from pan, remove foil and slice.

* Crush cookies in a zip-top plastic bag and then dispose of bag for easy clean up.

HINT: Keeps up to 2 months in the freezer.

SHREVES' BEST EVER FUDGE SAUCE

There are a couple of recipes in this book from Karen Shreves, a good friend of mine from way back. Karen always had ice cream in her freezer and this fudge sauce came in handy when she wanted a good treat to serve. You can't beat the flavor of this sauce. I have modified the recipe for the microwave to make it easier. This sauce is so much better than any you can buy at the grocery store.

Prep time: 3 min.	Microwave time: 2 min.	Quantity: approx. 1 cup

4 tablespoons all-purpose flour

¾ cup sugar

¼ cup cocoa

1 cup water

½ stick butter, ***room temperature***

⅛ teaspoon salt

1 teaspoon vanilla

1. In a large microwaveable bowl, combine flour, sugar and cocoa; add water. Whisk until smooth consistency, about 30 seconds.
2. Microwave on high for 2 minutes.
3. Remove from microwave immediately; whisk constantly for 1 minute.
4. Add butter, salt and vanilla; whisk until smooth.
5. Serve hot or cold over ice cream.

HINT: This sauce keeps in refrigerator for 3 weeks.

CARAMEL APPLE FLUFFY

My daughter, who can smell something sweet a mile away, thinks this is heaven on earth. Don't think of the calories—just the fun of serving it to the kids after a game.

Prep time: 10 min.   Bake time: none   Quantity: 10 servings

6 apples, peeled, cored, and chopped

1 can (20-ounce) crushed pineapple, drained

½ cup pecans, finely chopped (optional)

1 cup caramel apple dip (found in produce section)

1 container (8-ounce) non-dairy whipped topping, thawed

1. In a large bowl, combine apples, pineapple and pecans.
2. In a medium bowl, combine caramel apple dip and whipped topping; mix well. Pour over apple mixture; mix until combined.
3. Refrigerate until ready to serve.

HINT: You can serve 'fluffy' with additional nuts, cherries and drizzled caramel. Can be stored in refrigerator up to 3 days.

DESSERT DIP

This recipe came from a friend who made it for her family when they were growing up. It can be used when you have guests over and you don't want to serve the kids the Tiramisu dessert (which they probably won't like anyway).

Prep time: 5 min.	Cook time: none	Quantity: 2½ cups

Dip

1 box (3.4-ounce) chocolate instant pudding mix

2 cups cold milk

4 tablespoons peanut butter

Dipping Material

Marshmallows

Cookies

Fruit slices

Graham crackers

1. Prepare pudding as directed on package using milk in above recipe. Add peanut butter and combine until creamy; chill.
2. Pour into bowl and spread dipping material around dip; serve.
3. Can be made up to 3 days in advance.

HINT: If you are really pinched for time, you can always use the pre-made lunchbox puddings in place of the pudding mix.

TEST RESULTS: When I received this test page back from my neighbor, Shirley Sauer, it was splattered with chocolate everywhere. Written in big letters across the bottom of the page was "BIG HIT W/THE KIDS!" I knew this was good.

Index

got2go.

Index

Index

ORDER FORM

GOTAGO, LLC
P.O. Box 157
Okemos, Michigan 48805-0157

Feeding Families Fast

PLEASE SEND ME _____ copies of

Got 2 Go: Feeding Families Fast at $18.95 each .... $ _____

Add postage & handling $5.00 for first book .... $ _____

Add postage & handling for each additional book ($3.00 each) .... $ _____

Michigan residents add 6% sales tax .... $ _____

TOTAL .... $ _____

Name _____

Address _____

City _____ State _____ ZIP _____

Check or Money Order accepted – **Do not send cash**

Make check or money order payable to GOTAGO, LLC